Becker Gewers Kühn & Kühn Architekten

Hauptverwaltung der
Headquarters Building of
　　　　Verbundnetz Gas AG
　　　　Leipzig

Nordostansicht mit Konferenzturm.
View from north-east with conference tower.

Becker Gewers Kühn & Kühn Architekten

Hauptverwaltung der
Headquarters Building of
Verbundnetz Gas AG
Leipzig

Konzept und Text
Concept and text

Eike Becker

Prestel
München · London · New York

© Prestel Verlag, München · London · New York,
und Becker Gewers Kühn & Kühn Architekten, Berlin, 1999

Umschlag: Verbundnetz Gas AG Leipzig, Konferenzturm mit Lichtinstallation
von James Turrell, Foto: Jens Willebrand

Die Deutsche Bibliothek – CIP-Einheitsaufnahme
Hauptverwaltung der Verbundnetz Gas AG / Becker Gewers Kühn & Kühn Architekten.
Eike Becker. – München: Prestel, 1999
ISBN 3-7913-2130-7

Prestel Verlag, Mandlstraße 26, 80802 München
Telefon (089) 38 17 09-0, Fax (089) 38 17 09-35

Redaktion: Rudolf Stegers
Koordination: Johannes Determann
Übersetzung ins Englische: Peter Green

Fotografie: Blume, Bernd 76 (2); Schuller, Christian 6 (3), 7 (2), 8, 9 (2), 12, 13, 14 (2), 15 (3), 36, 61, 62, 66 (2); Wenzel, Falk 55, 56, 60, 64; Willebrand, Jens 2, 10, 16, 17, 23, 26, 27, 29 (4), 31, 32, 34, 35, 38, 39, 40, 42 (2), 43, 44, 45 (12), 46 (3), 47, 49, 50 (2), 52, 53 (3), 54, 59 (2), 63, 70 (8), 71 (8)

Gestaltung und Satz: xplicit ffm
Reproduktion: Repro Bayer, München
Druck und Bindung: Aumüller, Regensburg

Gedruckt auf chlorfrei gebleichtem Papier
Printed in Germany
ISBN 3-7913-2130-7

© Prestel Verlag, Munich · London · New York,
and Becker Gewers Kühn & Kühn Architects, Berlin, 1999

Cover: Verbundnetz Gas AG Leipzig, Conference tower with light installation
by James Turrell, photo: Jens Willebrand

Library of Congress Cataloging-in-Publication Data is available.

Prestel Verlag, Mandlstrasse 26, D-80802 Munich
Telephone +49 (89) 38 17 09-0, Fax +49 (89) 38 17 09-35
16 West 22nd Street, New York, NY 10010
Telephone +1 (212) 627 90 90, Fax +1 (212) 627 95 11
and 4 Bloomsbury Place, London WC1A2QA
Telephone +44 (171) 323 50 04, Fax +44 (171) 636 80 04

Prestel books are available worldwide.
Please contact your nearest bookseller
or write to one of the above addresses
for information concerning your local distributor.

Editing: Rudolf Stegers
Translation from the German: Peter Green
Coordination: Johannes Determann

Photography: Blume, Bernd 76 (2); Schuller, Christian 6 (3), 7 (2), 8, 9 (2), 12, 13, 14 (2), 15 (3), 36, 61, 62, 66 (2); Wenzel, Falk 55, 56, 60, 64; Willebrand, Jens 2, 10, 16, 17, 23, 26, 27, 29 (4), 31, 32, 34, 35, 38, 39, 40, 42 (2), 43, 44, 45 (12), 46 (3), 47, 49, 50 (2), 52, 53 (3), 54, 59 (2), 63, 70 (8), 71 (8)

Design and Typesetting: xplicit ffm
Lithography: Repro Bayer, Munich
Printing and Binding: Aumüller, Regensburg

Printed in Germany on acid-free paper
ISBN 3-7913-2130-7

Inhalt   Contents

6	Ankunft, rein und rauf	Arrival, entry, ascent
11	Platz und Berg und Tal	Space and hill and valley
14	Im Büro	Inside the office
18	Im Wandel	In transition
20	Auf der Briefmarke	Thumbnail design
22	Zwei in einem	Two in one
24	Aus eigener Kraft	Integral energy
26	Thermik	Thermal currents
28	Tragwerk	Load-bearing structure
30	Tag und Licht	Day and light
34	Haut und Hülle	Skin and enclosure
54	Macher oder Künstler	Doer or artist
56	Mit langem Atem	Staying power
60	Alles völlig anders	All totally different
64	Zucker, Peitsche & Jour fixe	Carrot, stick & talks
68	Licht Kunst Licht	Light art light
76	Daten und Fakten	Facts and figures
78	BGKK Biografien	BGKK biographies
80	Dank	Acknowledgements

Arrival, entry, ascent

Ankunft, rein und rauf

Berlin 1992/93. Auf dem Potsdamer Platz stehen Mauerreste, eine Aussichtsplattform und ein Souvenirladen. Unser Büro befindet sich im ehemaligen Grandhotel Esplanade…

Berlin, 1992–93. The remains of the Wall, an observation platform and a souvenir shop still stand on Potsdamer Platz. Our office is located in the former Grand Hotel Esplanade…

Das Grundstück befindet sich nordöstlich der Leipziger Innenstadt, mit dem Auto knapp 15 Minuten vom Hauptbahnhof entfernt. Es liegt an einer breiten Straße, in einem bis heute wenig entwickelten Gewerbepark, umgeben von Plattenbauten, Laubenpieperhütten, Einfamilienhäusern und ehemals genutzten Industrieanlagen. Als die Bauarbeit für die Hauptverwaltung der Verbundnetz Gas AG begann, war der Ort eher durch Vorstellungen und Erwartungen als durch seine wirkliche Erscheinung bestimmt. In diesem noch labilen Areal wollten wir ein markantes Gebäude schaffen.

Von der Bautzener Straße in die Braunstraße biegend, fährt man an einer sechs Geschosse hohen, langen gläsernen Fassade vorbei, bevor man links die Einfahrt des Grundstücks erreicht. Der Weg führt um den transparenten Konferenzturm, vorbei an einem

The site lies to the north-east of the city centre of Leipzig, barely 15 minutes by car from the main station. Situated on a wide road in a commercial park that has remained relatively undeveloped up to the present, the complex is surrounded by a variety of structures: buildings in prefabricated panel construction, allotments and huts, single-family houses, and disused industrial plants. When the construction of the headquarters for the Verbundnetz Gas AG began, the location was defined more by visions and expectations than by its actual appearance. It was our aim to create a building with a striking form in this somewhat amorphous area.

Turning from Bautzener Straße into Braunstraße, visitors drive past a long six-storey glazed façade before reaching the entrance to the site on the left.

...Bauherrenbesprechungen führen wir im Kaisersaal durch, der später von Sony als Ganzes verschoben wurde.

...Discussions with the clients were conducted in the Kaisersaal, which was later moved by Sony en bloc to a different location.

8 Ankunft, rein und rauf | Arrival, entry, ascent

Gemeinschaften haben einen Marktplatz, an dem sie zusammenkommen und am Leben der anderen teilnehmen. Das Gespräch von Gesicht zu Gesicht ist Voraussetzung für Vitalität.

Communities have a forum where they can come together and participate in the lives of others. Face-to-face communication is essential to vitality.

flachen Wasserbecken und der Nordwand, hinter deren großen Scheiben das lichte Atrium mit Bäumen, Rolltreppen und zwei gestuften Terrassen in den Blick kommen. Dann um das wie eine Hand gekrümmte, mit Aluminium geschlossene Treppenhaus und links zu den beiden Drehtüren des Eingangs unter dem ovalen Vordach aus Stahl und Glas.

Durch das Foyer mit der Loge für den Pförtner nach vorn rechts in das Atrium. Dann schräg rechts die Rolltreppen hinauf und durch das offene Restaurant weiter bis an die Südwand und fast unter das Dach. Wer sich umdreht, hat links und rechts je einen Büroriegel, hinten die Südwand, vorne die Nordwand. Der Blick schweift: von Kathedralwand zu Kathedralwand, über die Kaskade der Terrassen, von oben nach unten, durch die ganze Länge des Hauses. 151 200 Kubikmeter Bruttorauminhalt, 32 800 Quadratmeter Bruttogeschoßfläche.

The route leads round the transparent conference tower, past a shallow pool of water and along the north face of the building. Through the large glass panes of this façade, visitors catch a glimpse of the brightly lit atrium with its trees, escalators and two terraced levels. The path continues round an aluminium-clad staircase element, folded like a hand, and turns left to the two revolving doors of the entrance set beneath an oval canopy of steel and glass.

Passing through the foyer with the doorkeeper's lodge, visitors have a view of the atrium to the right, where the route continues obliquely up the escalators and through an open restaurant that extends to the south wall and almost up to the roof. Turning round to face the north wall again, one finds oneself flanked by office tracts left and right. The view stetches from "cathedral wall" to "cathedral wall", over the cascading terraces, from top to bottom of the space, through the entire length of the building, which has an overall volume of 151,200 cubic metres, and a gross floor area of 32,800 square metres.

Gewerbepark Leipzig Nordost. Die Ränder fransen aus und verwischen die Grenze zwischen Stadt und Land.

Commercial Park North-East Leipzig. The edges fray out; the boundary between city and country dissolves.

Der Blick nach Norden durch die Kathedralwand über den »Reflecting Pool« verbindet Innen und Außen.

The view to the north through the "cathedral wall" and across the reflecting pool establishes a link between indoors and outdoors.

Place and hill and valley

Between the two office tracts – four storeys high to the west, six storeys high to the east – it is above all the sense of space that impresses itself on visitors. To the north, a glass façade rises from floor to ceiling. To the south is the rear face behind the stepped terraces and the computer areas; and between the two, a stream of light and air; people coming and going; encounters – spontaneous and planned – between members of the staff; and now and then, meetings with clients. Altogether, there is a convivial atmosphere, a sense of togetherness; even celebrations may be held here, such as the New Year's Eve party at the end of 1999.

The space, 17.5 m wide and 75 m long, leads in a single, gradual upward movement from the depths to the heights – from valley to hilltop. It rises from the placid pool of water in front of the north face, through the skin of glass into the atrium and up the three-storey cascade of steps – not unlike the Spanish Steps in Rome – to the spacious restaurant and the roof garden that commands a view south towards the station and the city centre.

Within the internal space, the individual architectural elements are restrained, subordinated to the overall design. Furnishings and reception counter stand ready to welcome clients and guests. The lush-green olive trees are the most important feature of the interior design. The pavings are in Blanco Castilia granite; linking the office tracts are narrow bridges, where the route leads over panels of matt glass 1.5 x 1 m in size. In the east wing, a gallery with a glass balustrade extends from north to south. The visitor comes to a halt. His eyes roam over the broad west wall on the opposite side. Visible behind the finely articulated grid of glass panels are potted plants, desks and monitors, brightly lit and darker office spaces, people sitting or standing, working at the keyboard, speaking on the phone, or in the middle of a conversation perhaps.

Platz und Berg und Tal

Zwischen den beiden Büroflügeln mit vier Geschossen im Westen und sechs Geschossen im Osten ist es vor allem: frei. Im Norden vom Boden zur Decke eine gläserne Fassade, im Süden die Rückseite des Stufenbergs mit den Rechnern, dazwischen ein Strom von Licht und Luft, Kommen und Gehen von Menschen, Begegnungen von Angestellten aus Absicht oder Zufall. Dann und wann auch Treffen mit Kunden, geselliges Beisammensein, Feste gar. Silvester 1999!

17,5 Meter breit und 75 Meter lang, führt der Raum in einer einzigen langsamen Bewegung aus der Tiefe in die Höhe, vom Tal zum Berg. Von der stillen Wasserfläche vor der Nordwand durch deren Glas in das Atrium, über die drei Geschosse des Stufenbaus, einer »Spanischen Treppe« verwandt, hinauf zum geräumigen Restaurant und zur Terrasse mit Blick nach Süden, Richtung Bahnhof und Altstadt.

Die Architekturelemente des Innenraumes halten sich zurück. Überall bestimmt das Gesamte das Einzelne. Möbel und Theke stehen bereit zum Empfang der Kunden und Gäste. Die sattgrünen Olivenbäume sind das wichtigste Stück des Interior Design. Der Boden besteht aus hellgrauem Blanco-Castilia-Granit. Die Büroriegel verbinden schmale Brücken. Man geht dort über matte Glasfelder von 1,5 mal 1 Meter. Im Ostflügel erstreckt sich von Nord nach Süd eine Galerie mit einer Brüstung aus Glas. Man bleibt stehen. Die Augen streifen über die breite Westwand vis-à-vis. Hinter dem feinen Raster der Scheiben die Topfblumen, die Schreibtische, die Bildschirme, die helleren und dunkleren Büros, die Menschen im Sitzen und Stehen, vor einer Tastatur, an einem Telefon. Vielleicht mitten im Gespräch.

Terrassen, Rolltreppen und Brücken machen den Raum von unten und oben erlebbar. Sie erschließen die Etagen.

Terraces, escalators and bridges not only link the various levels. Whether viewed from above or below, they heighten the sense of space.

Im Büro

Trotz großer Flexibilität durch neueste Informations- und Kommunikationstechnologien heißt Büroarbeit noch immer und vor allem: Arbeit an einem festen Ort zu einer festen Zeit. Tagaus tagein ist in der Hauptverwaltung der Verbundnetz Gas AG ein halbes Tausend Menschen tätig. Die Gestaltung ihrer Arbeitsplätze war Anliegen des Vorstands, des Betriebsrats, des Nutzerausschusses, der Bildschirmarbeitsgruppe, des Beauftragten für Arbeitssicherheit, des Betriebsarztes.

Bei den Angestellten spielte der Wunsch nach dem eigenen Arbeitsplatz eine große Rolle. Daher entschied sich der Nutzer für den Bau von Zellen- und Gruppenbüros. Das Regelbüro im Normalgeschoß der beiden Flügel hat 24 Quadratmeter mit einem Raster von 1,5 Metern und einer Höhe von 3 Metern. Jeder Raum ist für zwei Mitarbeiter eingerichtet, doch lassen sich die Zwischenwände mühelos versetzen, jeder Raum mühelos erweitern. Die Leuchten folgen dem Raster und hängen lotrecht zur Fassade. Innerhalb eines festen Möbelprogramms konnten die Angestellten sich für eine bestimmte Ausstattung entscheiden.

Die im Zusammenhang offener Konzepte häufig diskutierten Nachteile von Zellenbüros treten bei diesem Neubau in den Hintergrund, da durch die Terrassen und das Restaurant im Atrium für die eher informelle Kommunikation viel Platz vorhanden ist. Für eine eher formelle Besprechung in kleinerer oder größerer Runde stehen eigens Räume zur Verfügung. Im Westflügel öffnen sich diese Räume sämtlich zu Balkonen und Terrassen.

Doppelböden im Mittelbereich der Geschoßdecken und Hohlraumböden mit Bodenauslässen erleichtern die technische Versorgung.

Despite the great degree of flexibility afforded by state-of-the-art information and communications technology, most office work still means employment in a fixed place at a fixed time. Day after day, some 500 people are working in the Verbundnetz Gas AG administration. The design of their workplaces was the concern of the board, the staff council, the user committee, the computer working group, the works safety representative and the company doctor.

The wish of the employees for personalized workplaces played a major role. The tenant therefore decided in favour of a design with single and group offices. The typical office spaces on the standard floors in the two wings of the building have an area of 24 square metres each and a clear height of 3 metres. They are laid out on a 1.5-metre grid. Each space is designed for two persons. The partitions can, however, be moved without difficulty, so that the individual rooms can easily be extended. The lighting installation follows the same grid, with linear ceiling fittings laid out at right angles to the façade. Members of the staff were able to select individual furnishings from a fixed programme.

The much-discussed disadvantages of individual office cells in comparison with open-plan concepts have little relevance in this development, since the terrace areas and the restaurant in the atrium provide a great deal of space for informal communication. More formal discussions, in larger or smaller groups, are held in rooms specially created for that purpose. In the west wing, these spaces all open on to balconies or terraces.

The installation of services is facilitated by the double-floor construction in the central areas and by hollow floors with outlets. During the installation of glass-fibre cables, phone and fax

Heute können viele frei entscheiden, mit wem sie wann und wo arbeiten möchten. Zellenbüros konkurrieren erfolgreich mit Werkstatt- und Clubbüros.

Nowadays, there is greater scope for employees to decide when, where and with whom they wish to work. Individual office units compete successfully with workshop and club-type offices.

Inside the office

Die Jalousien richten sich nach dem Stand der Sonne. Je nach Bedarf reflektieren sie das Licht in das Innere oder halten die Strahlung fern.

The blinds react to the position of the sun, deflecting light into the interior of the building or screening off insolation, as required.

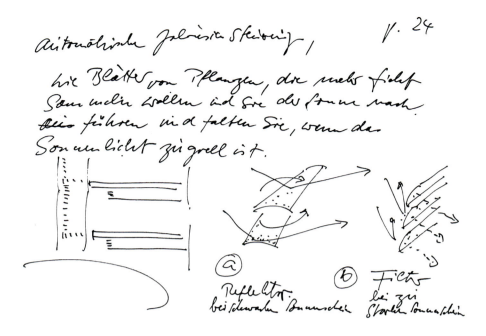

Blick aus dem Atrium in das Café im vierten Obergeschoß.

View from the atrium to the fourth-floor café.

Beim Verkabeln mit Glasfasern wurden die Leitungen für Telefon und Telefax und die Leitungen für Daten voneinander getrennt. Das Firmennetz ermöglicht betriebliche Ferngespräche zu allen Standorten des Unternehmens. Alle Personal Computer sind miteinander verbunden. Desk sharing wäre möglich.

Über ein Metallpaneel im Türrahmen können Lichtstärke, Sonnenschutz, Wärme und Kühle im Raum je nach eigenem Befinden reguliert werden. Erst nach Feierabend übernimmt das digitale Leitsystem des Gebäudes die technische Steuerung der Büros und optimiert den Verbrauch von Energie. Das Licht geht aus. Die Heizung auch. Die Jalousien öffnen oder schließen sich. Bis zum nächsten Tage ...

installations were laid separately from those for data communications. A company network allows long-distance calls to be made to all offices belonging to the concern; all PCs are networked. A desk-sharing system is a further option.

From a metal panel in the door frames, lighting intensity, sun-screening, heating and cooling can be regulated within the office spaces according to individual needs. Only after office hours does the building's digital control and instrumentation system come into operation to monitor the technical systems within the offices, thus optimizing the consumption of energy. The lights are turned off, the heating is turned down, and the blinds are opened or closed – until the following day.

Schnitt durch den östlichen Büroflügel mit Klimafassade links, Atriumfassade rechts und Mittelgang.

Section through eastern office wing with double façade on the left, the central corridor, and the atrium façade on the right.

Deckenspiegel mit integrierten Leuchten, Sprinklerköpfen, Kühlelementen in den Büros, Aluminiumpaneeldecke mit einseitiger Wandbeleuchtung im Mittelgang.

Ceiling plan, showing integrated lighting, sprinklers and cooling elements in the offices. Central corridor with aluminium soffit panels and wall lighting on one side.

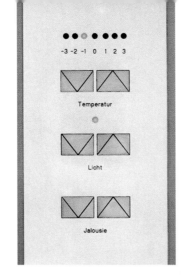

Bedienpaneel im Türrahmen. Von einem Rechner, der auch außerhalb des Gebäudes stehen könnte, werden Heizung, Kühlung, Lüftung und Sanitärtechnik optimiert.

Control panel in door frame. Heating, cooling, ventilation and sanitary technology are optimized by a computer installation that could also be located outside the building.

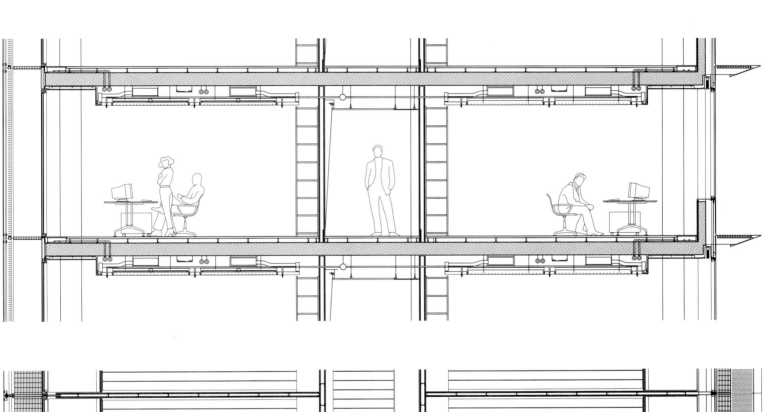

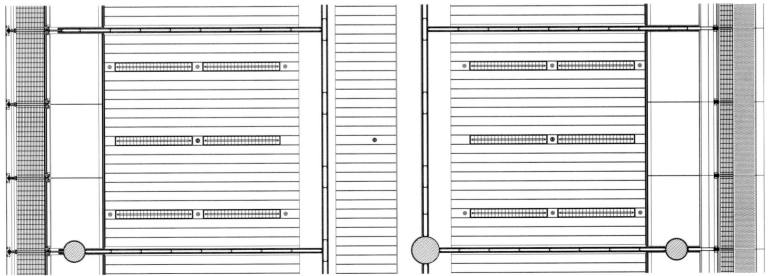

17

In Europe and America, we are witnessing the disappearance of industrial societies, the development of information and service societies and the emergence of a society of knowledge.

New strategies are replacing old concepts, and that is why our building has to be flexible. It must be capable of change, of adaptation when circumstances or its users so require. Something that has long applied to any good computer is increasingly coming to apply to architecture: its software and hardware need to be upgraded from time to time. The potential for extension and improvement has to be present when a building is completed; for work is subject to a process of change. Tomorrow is not today.

In transition

Wir sehen in Europa und Amerika die Industriegesellschaft verschwinden, die Informations- und Servicegesellschaft aufsteigen und die Wissensgesellschaft kommen.

Neue Strategien ersetzen alte Konzeptionen. Daher soll unser Gebäude beweglich sein. Es muß sich verändern, muß sich anpassen können, wenn die Umstände es fordern und die Benutzer es wollen. Was für jeden guten Computer längst gilt, gilt mehr und mehr auch für die Architektur: Ihre Soft- und Hardware brauchen Upgrades. Das Potential für Erweiterung und Verbesserung muß schon bei der Fertigstellung vorhanden sein. Denn Arbeit ist im Wandel. Morgen ist nicht heute.

Thumbnail design

Auf der Briefmarke

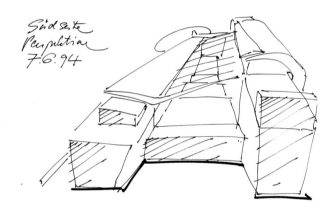

Mit groben, oft nur sehr kleinen Skizzen und mit einfachen Modellen entwickeln wir unsere ersten Ideen und Konzepte. Zahlreiche Diagramme und Schemata, etwa zur Organisation des Gebäudes, treten in einen Wettbewerb. Zunächst soll alles so einfach wie möglich sein. Man muß es schon auf den ersten Blick verstehen können. Mit der äußeren und inneren Gestaltung, mit leichten oder schweren Körpern, mit Textur und Objekt, mit bestimmten Materialien und Konstruktionen, kurz: mit Architektur, hat das noch wenig zu tun. Die Form halten wir aus diesem Prozeß lange fern.

We develop our initial ideas and concepts by means of rough, often tiny, sketches and simple models. Numerous diagrams and schematic ideas vie with each other; for example, in determining the organization of the building. At the outset, everything should be as simple as possible, so that it can be understood at a glance. All this has little to do with the actual external or internal design, with lightweight or heavy volumes, with texture and object, with different materials or forms of construction - in other words, with the architectural content. We keep the question of form out of this process for a long time.

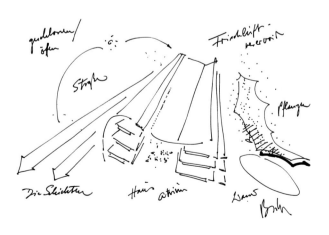

Entwurfsskizze mit der Disposition der Elemente Büroflügel, Atrium und Stufenberg.

Design sketch, showing layout of main elements: office tracts, atrium and cascade of stairs.

Die bewegte Gebäudehülle verbindet beide Teile. Unter dem Glasdach liegt der Marktplatz, darunter geschützt das Rechenzentrum.

The outer enclosure with its lively irregular form unites the two parts of the building. Beneath the glass roof is the forum or marketplace, which is situated protectively over the computer control centre.

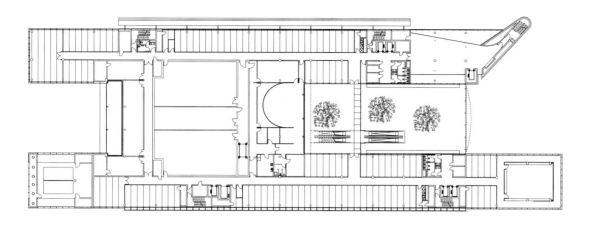

Erstes Obergeschoß. Der Westflügel wird durch die Diagonale des Eingangsbereichs, der Ostflügel durch den fast quadratischen Konferenzturm geprägt.

First floor plan. The western tract is dominated by the diagonal lines of the entrance area, the eastern tract by the cubic conference tower.

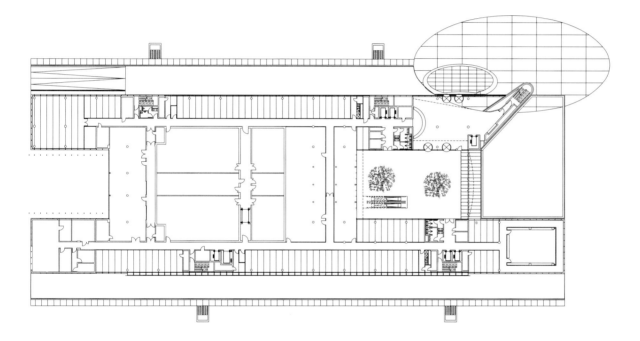

Erdgeschoß. Den Eingang markieren ein ovaler Vorplatz und ein ovales Vordach. Zwischen den Büroflügeln liegen das Atrium und das Rechenzentrum.

Ground floor plan. The entrance is approached via an oval apron area with an oval canopy. Situated between the office tracts are the atrium and the computer centre.

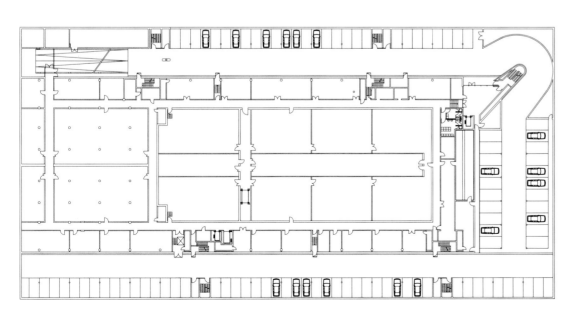

Untergeschoß. In der Mitte liegen Rechenzentrum und Energiezentrale. Außen befinden sich 97 Stellplätze, die über eine Rampe an der Südwestecke erreichbar sind.

Basement plan. The central area is occupied by the computer centre and the energy control plant. Around the edges are 97 parking spaces, which are reached via a ramp at the south-west corner of the complex.

Zwei in einem
Two in one

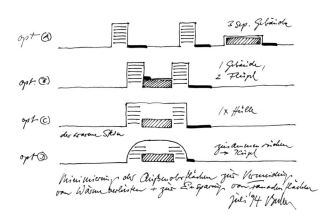

Das von der Josef Esch Fonds Projekt GmbH und der Verbundnetz Gas AG gemeinsam erstellte Raumprogramm war schon im Ansatz ungewöhnlich. Es handelt sich einerseits um ein typisches Verwaltungsgebäude für etwa 550 Angestellte in Büroräumen, andererseits um ein spezielles Rechenzentrum, von dem aus die Gasversorgung der sechs östlichen Bundesländer gesteuert wird.

Die Verbindung zweier so unterschiedlicher Nutzungen machte eine Symbiose möglich. Beide Teile, der Verwaltungsbau und das Rechenzentrum, sind energetisch und organisatorisch miteinander verbunden. Beide Teile profitieren voneinander. Die empfindlichen Steuerungsanlagen ruhen wie ein großer warmer Stein in der Mitte des Hauses unter den Terrassen des Atriums. Das Rechenzentrum gibt den Büroflügeln Wärme. Die Büroflügel geben dem Rechenzentrum Schutz.

The spatial programme drawn up jointly by the Josef Esch Fonds Projekt GmbH and the Verbundnetz Gas AG was unusual in its concept. On the one hand, a typical administration building was required for roughly 550 employees working in offices; on the other hand, a special computer centre was to be installed, from where the gas supply to the six eastern federal states of Germany could be controlled.

The combination of two quite different functions such as these made it necessary to seek a state of symbiosis. Both sections – the administration areas and the computer centre – are linked with each other in terms of energy use and organization. Each part profits from the other. The sensitive control plant is situated like a large warm stone at the heart of the building, beneath the atrium terraces. The computer centre provides warmth for the office tracts; and the office tracts provide protection for the computer centre.

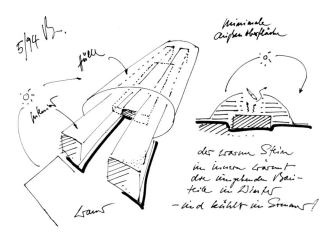

Die Verbindung von Büroflächen und Rechenzentrum sowie deren Umhüllung vermindern den Wärmeverlust.

Heat losses were reduced by linking the office areas and the computer centre and enclosing them within a single skin.

Im Querschnitt werden die Formen der beiden Dächer als eine fließende Bewegung erkennbar.

In cross-section, the forms of the two parts of the roof can be recognized as a flowing movement.

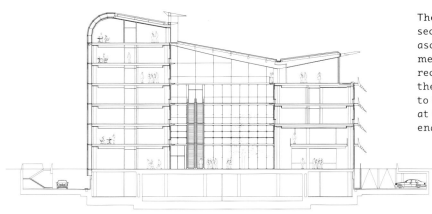

Der Längsschnitt zeigt die steigende Bewegung vom Empfangsbereich im Norden zum Restaurant im Süden.

The longitudinal section shows the ascending movement from the reception area at the northern end to the restaurant at the southern end.

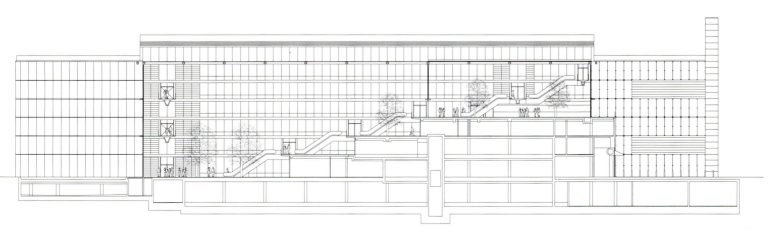

Integral energy

Aus eigener Kraft

»Wenn die Kleidung eine Ausweitung unserer eigenen Haut zur Speicherung und Verteilung unserer Körperwärme und Energie darstellt, so ist die Wohnung ein Kollektivmittel zur Erreichung desselben Zieles für die Familie oder Gruppe. Die Wohnung als Schutz ist eine Ausweitung des Wärmehaushaltsmechanismus unseres Körpers, eine Kollektivhaut, ein Gemeinschaftskleid.«

Marshall McLuhan,
Die magischen Kanäle, 1964

In der Verbundnetz Gas AG hatten wir einen Partner, der sich für unsere Vorstellung von Ökologie und Architektur, von Natur und Technik, von Nachhaltigkeit und von größten Wirkungen durch kleinste Eingriffe rasch anregen und begeistern ließ. Als Lieferant von Energie muß sich das Unternehmen diesen Problemen ohnehin stellen. Für den Entwurf des Leipziger Gebäudes mußten wir auf zwei Fragen eine Antwort suchen.

Erstens: Wieviel Energie benötigt man vor Ort, um dort Wärme und Kälte zu erzeugen?

Zweitens: Wieviel Kohlendioxid wird dabei an die Umwelt abgegeben?

Die Idee, den Verwaltungsbau und das Rechenzentrum nicht allein räumlich, sondern auch in bezug auf Heizung und Kühlung des Neubaus zu verbinden, setzte starke Synergien frei.

Die vor allem für das Rechenzentrum benötigte Energie wird vor Ort durch mehrere Blockheizkraftwerke (BHKW) produziert. Im Winter wird die Abwärme dieser Anlagen zum Heizen der Büros und des Atriums genutzt. Im Sommer wird die Abwärme mit Hilfe von Absorptionskältemaschinen zum Kühlen verwandt. Dabei ist die Systemgrenze nicht gleich der Grundstücksgrenze. Auch die Schadstoffe der Kraftwerke, die das Gebäude unter Umständen von außen versorgen, fließen in die Bewertung ein.

Die dezentralen BHKW werden mit Erdgas gespeist, das im Vergleich zu Kohle und Öl den Ausstoß von Kohlendioxid um 30 bis 50 Prozent senkt. Die BHKW haben einen extrem hohen elektrischen Wirkungsgrad, weil die Energie innerhalb des Gebäudes bleibt, also kein Verlust durch Transport entsteht. Der Wirkungsgrad der Leipziger Anlagen beträgt 85 Prozent, während er sich bei den meisten heutigen Kraftwerken nur auf 40 Prozent beläuft. Zusätzlich besteht die Möglichkeit einer Ausspeisung von Energie an die Stadt.

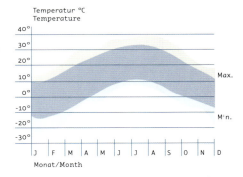

Jahrestemperatur Leipzig
Annual Temperature Levels

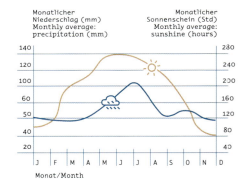

Sonnenschein/Niederschlag Leipzig
Annual Sunshine/Precipitation

Wir versuchen, unsere Gebäude in energetische Kreisläufe einzubinden. Voraussetzung ist die Analyse der Umgebung.

We attempt to integrate our buildings into energy cycles. This requires a close analysis of the surrounding environment.

In his book "Understanding Media: The Extensions of Man" (1964), Marshall McLuhan wrote that if clothing represents an extension of our own skin, a means of storing and distributing our body heat and energy, the dwelling is a collective means of achieving the same goal for the family or other human group. The dwelling, as a protective enclosure, is an extension of the mechanism controlling the thermal balance of our body: a collective skin, a communal article of attire, so to speak.

The Verbundnetz Gas AG was a partner that very quickly showed a great enthusiasm for our concept of ecology and architecture, nature and technology, sustainability and maximum effect with a minimum use of resources. The company allowed itself to be inspired by this concept. As an energy supplier, it is automatically confronted with issues of this kind anyway. For the design of the building in Leipzig, we had to seek answers to two important questions.

First, how much energy would be needed in this location for the required heating and cooling?

Second, how much carbon dioxide would be emitted into the atmosphere as a result of this?

The idea of linking the administration tract with the computer centre, not only spatially, but in respect of the heating and cooling systems, led to a powerful expression of synergy.

The energy required above all for the computer centre is produced on site by a number of co-generating units (local heating and power blocks). In winter, waste heat from these units is used to heat the offices and the atrium. In summer, waste heat is used for cooling, with the aid of adsorption cooling machines. The system boundaries do not coincide with the site boundaries. Conversely, pollution from external power stations that may serve the building under certain circumstances also has to be taken into account in evaluating the system.

The decentralized co-generating units are fuelled by natural gas, which, compared with to coal and oil, reduces the emission of carbon dioxide by 30–50 per cent. The co-generating units have an extremely high electrical efficiency, since the energy remains within the building and there are no losses through transport. The efficiency of the plant in Leipzig is 85 per cent, compared with only 40 per cent for most power stations today. In addition, there is scope for supplying excess energy to the city.

Aus der Mehrfach-nutzung der Abwärme bei der Stromer-zeugung resultiert die größte Einsparung von Energie.

The greatest energy saving results from the multiple use of waste heat from power generation.

Jahresenergieverbrauch (MWh/a)
Annual energy consumption (MWh/a)

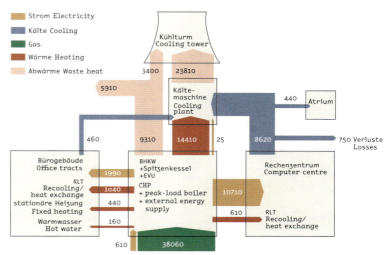

Aufteilung des Energieverbrauchs
Breakdown of annual energy consumption

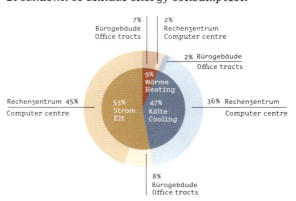

Thermik   Thermal currents

Der Windkanal mit dem Luftleitflügel läuft über die Länge des Atriumdaches. Von Osten kommend, streicht der Wind über die gekrümmte Klimafassade. Er erzeugt unter dem Flügel einen Druck. So wird die natürliche Entlüftung des Atriumraumes unterstützt.

The air conduit with the wind deflector above it extends over the length of the atrium roof. Easterly winds flow over the curved climate-control façade and around the deflector, creating a zone of increased air pressure beneath it and thereby supporting the natural ventilation of the atrium space.

Bei der Formgebung des Gebäudes spielte die natürliche Thermik innerhalb und außerhalb des Atriums eine wichtige Rolle. Es kam darauf an, den Luftstrom im Sommer für die Auskühlung, im Winter für die Erwärmung des Hauses zu nutzen.

Im Sommer unterstützt das Atrium die Lüftung der Büros. Am Tag steigt erwärmte Luft aus dem großen Binnenhof und Stufenberg auf, entweicht durch einen Windkanal im Dach und zieht verbrauchte Luft aus den Büros nach. Nachts streicht kühle Luft durch die Öffnungen der gläsernen nördlichen und südlichen Fassade über die Speichermasse der Atriumterrassen. Heizung und Kühlung unter den Bodenplatten stärken diesen Tag- und Nachteffekt.

Im Winter scheint die Sonne durch die Südwand und das Glasdach und erwärmt das Atrium sowie die Büros.

In the formal design of the building, natural thermal behaviour inside and outside the atrium played an important role. The aim was to use air currents for cooling in summer and for warming the building in winter.

In summer, the atrium supports the natural ventilation of the offices. During the day, warmed air rises from the large internal space and the stepped terraces, passes through a conduit in the roof and draws vitiated air out of the offices in its wake. At night, cool air flows through the openings in the glazed north and south façades and over the thermal storage mass of the atrium terraces. Heating and cooling installations beneath the floor slabs reinforce this day-and-night effect.

In winter, the sun shines through the south face of the building and the glass roof and warms the atrium and the offices.

Natürliche Lüftung des Atriums
Natural Ventilation of the Atrium

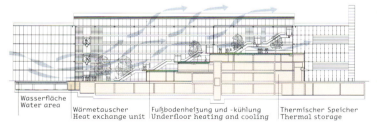

Wasserfläche / Water area
Wärmetauscher / Heat exchange unit
Fußbodenheizung und -kühlung / Underfloor heating and cooling
Thermischer Speicher / Thermal storage

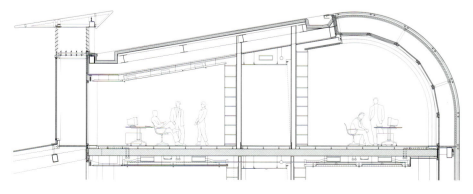

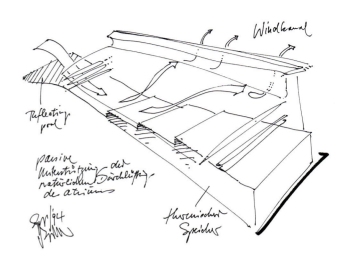
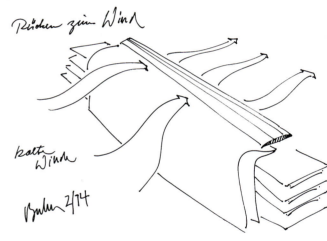
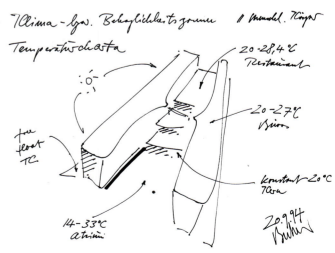

Tragwerk   Load-bearing structure

1 Handlauf, Aluminium-
strangpreßprofil,
natureloxiert

2 Eingespannte Glas-
brüstung, ESG 12 mm

3 VSG Bodenplatten,
bedruckt

4 Natursteinplatten,
Blanco Castillia

5 Stahlkragarm als
Unterkonstruktion

1 natural-anodized
aluminium handrail

2 12 mm toughened
safety glass balu-
strade, rigidly fixed

3 laminated safety
glass floor panels
with printed surface

4 Blanco Castilia
granite paving slabs

5 steel cantilevered
supporting bracket

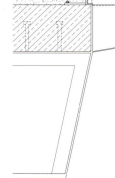

Querschnitt durch
eine Brücke. Ein-
gespannte gläser-
ne Brüstungen und
begehbare Glas-
flächen lassen sie
leicht erscheinen.

Section through
one of the brid-
ges. Rigidly fixed
glass balustrades
together with
glass pavings
create an impres-
sion of lightness.

Die Hauptverwaltung der Verbundnetz Gas AG ist ein Stahlbetonbau.
Das Stützenraster beträgt 7,5
mal 5,0 und 7,5 mal 7,5 Meter.
Die Geschoßdecken bestehen aus
27 Zentimeter starken Flach-
deckenplatten. Die Dehnfuge quer
durch das Haus minimiert die
Gefahr von Rissen aufgrund thermischer Bedingungen. Im Inneren
des Gebäudes bilden die Rund-
stützen aus Stahlbeton einen
deutlichen Gegensatz zu den
weißen Wänden.

Die vierten bis sechsten Geschosse, die Fassaden des Atriums
sowie das Flügeldach sind reiner
Stahlbau. Die Hauptträger des
Flügeldachs haben einen Abstand
von 7,5 Meter. Am östlichen Büroriegel geht straßenseitig die Wand
durch die Rundung nahtlos in das
Dach über. Rahmen und Binder
ruhen auf dem Stützenraster.
Pfetten spannen im Abstand von
bis zu drei Meter.

The headquarters building
of the Verbundnetz Gas AG has a
reinforced concrete structure.
The columns are laid out to 7.5 x
5.0 metre and 7.5 x 7.5 metre grids.
The floors consist of 27-centi-
metre flat slabs. An expansion
joint running through the entire
structure minimizes the danger
of thermal cracking. Inside the
building, the circular reinforced
concrete columns form a striking
contrast to the white walls.

The structure of the fourth to
sixth floors, the façades to the
atrium, and the wing-like roof
are all in steel construction.
The frames and roof girders are
supported by the grid of columns.
The main girders of the wing-like
roof are at 7.5-metre centres; and
the purlins in the longitudinal
direction are laid out at up
to 3-metre centres. The street
façade at the top of the eastern
office tract merges in a con-
tinuous curve with the roof.

Die Kathedralwände,
das Glasdach und
die Brücken sind
gelenkige Stahl-
konstruktionen.
Ihre Formen passen
sich dem Momenten-
verlauf an.

The cathedral walls,
the glass roof and
the bridges are in
a hinged steel con-
struction. Their
forms reflect the
bending moment
line.

Day and light

Tag und Licht

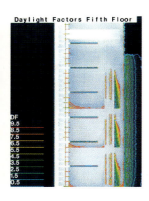

Die Tageslichtverhältnisse im Atrium und den angrenzenden Büros wurden während der Planung berechnet.

Daylight conditions within the atrium and the adjoining offices were calculated during the planning stage.

Im Bürobau hat sich die Lichtplanung schon während der achtziger Jahre von der Elektroplanung getrennnt. Bei den Konzepten für Tages- und für Kunstlicht haben wir mit George Sexton zusammengearbeitet. Ziel war die Ganzheitlichkeit von Licht und Architektur. Der Raum leuchtet von sich aus. Außen gliedert das Kunstlicht den Bau, innen rhythmisiert es das Gebäude durch den Wechsel von wärmeren und kühleren Räumen.

Von der Straße aus betrachtet, führt die Beleuchtung der Büroräume das Auge von der gläsernen Fassade wie durch Reihen von Fächern in die Tiefe des Gebäudes. Mal eher weiß und linear, mal eher gelb und punktuell, wird der Raum innen durch Licht moduliert. Weiß wirkt es in den Büros, gelb in den Lobbys, vor den Aufzügen sowie in den beiden obersten Geschossen. Auf den Terrassen des Atriums hingegen erscheint das Kunstlicht wie Tageslicht.

As early as the 1980s, lighting design in office construction became a discipline in its own right, distinct from the general electrical planning. In drawing up concepts for the natural and artificial lighting of the present complex, we collaborated with George Sexton. Our aim was to unite light and architecture to create a homogeneous whole. The spaces radiate from within. Externally, artificial light is used to articulate the building. Internally, it establishes an alternating rhythm of warmer and cooler spaces.

Seen from the road, the artificial lighting in the offices leads the eye from the glazed façade through a series of layers and compartments into the depths of the building. White and linear in places, yellow and point-like in others, the lighting modulates the internal spaces. In the offices, it appears white; in the lobbies, in front of the lifts and on the two uppermost floors, it is yellow. On the atrium terraces, the artificial lighting has a daylight quality.

An der Ostfassade unterscheidet die Lichtfarbe das oberste von den übrigen Geschossen.

The lighting coloration on the east face of the building differentiates the topmost storeys from the lower floors.

Für das Kunstlicht in den Büros wurden unterschiedliche Konzepte simuliert. Die achsenbezogene Beleuchtung quer zur Fassade bietet die beste Lösung: gleichmäßige Ausleuchtung von 500 Lux im Durchschnitt, Blendfreiheit und Tiefenbezug.

All kinds of artificial lighting concepts were simulated for the offices. An axial layout at right angles to the façade proved to be the best solution, providing an even, full degree of lighting without glare and extending into the depths of the spaces. The average level of illumination is 500 lux.

Skin and enclosure

Zweimal im Jahr werden die Fassaden gereinigt.

The façades are cleaned twice a year.

Haut und Hülle

Bereits beim Wettbewerb 1992 hatten wir das Gebäude mit doppelter Fassade entworfen. Damals stand die Diskussion um die Klimamembran noch am Anfang. Üblich war, daß von Architekten entworfene gläserne Fassaden mit Handwerkern geplant und gebaut wurden. An der Entwicklung neuer Fassadensysteme arbeiten heute Fachleute für Tragwerke und Baustoffe, Spezialisten für Thermik und Elektrik, Berater für Sicherheit und Brandschutz, Experten für Computersimulationen und Windkanalversuche.

Fassaden verstehen wir einerseits als informative Filter, andererseits als klimatische Membrane. Wie bei Mensch und Tier sind bei diesem Gebäude die Hautschichten jeweils für ihre Aufgabe geschaffen. Jedes der neun verwendeten Fassadensysteme wurde eigens für dieses Vorhaben entwickelt und verwirklicht: an der Straßenseite im Osten eine Doppelfassade, an der Gartenseite im Westen eine Fassade mit festem äußeren Sonnenschutz und großen Schiebefenstern, an der Nord- und Südfassade sowie am Konferenzturm eine geschoßhohe Pfosten-Riegel-Konstruktion, am Klimaturm Planarglas, am Haupteingang

As early as 1992, in the course of the competition, we designed a building with a double-façade construction. At that time, the whole discussion about climate-control membranes was just beginning. It was common for a glazed façade designed by an architect to be planned and realized in collaboration with the trade firms that would subsequently execute the work. Today, experts in load-bearing structures and materials, electrical specialists, security and fire-protection consultants, and professionals in thermal currents, computer simulation and wind-tunnel testing are all likely to be involved in the development of new façade systems.

We understand façades as information filters and as climatic membranes. As in the case of the human body or the bodies of animals, the various layers of the skin of this building were created to fulfil specific functions. Each of the nine façade systems used in the scheme was specially designed for this project. Along the street face on the eastern side of the building is a double-layer façade. The garden face to the west has a façade with fixed

eine Rain-Screen-Fassade, im Atrium an der West- und Ostseite eine Pfosten-Riegel-Konstruktion mit Akustiksegeln, im Atrium an den Terrassen eine Sicherheitsverglasung, in der Leitwarte des Rechenzentrums elektrochromatische Glaswände, in den Konferenzbereichen eine Flush-Glazing-Fassade mit Jalousien.

external sunscreen elements and large sliding windows. The façades to the north and south ends and to the conference tower are in a storey-height post-and-rail construction. The climate-control tower is clad in planar glass elements. At the main entrance, there is a rain-screen façade, and on the west and east sides of the atrium are post-and-rail façades with acoustic sails. The terraces of the atrium are clad in safety glass. Electrochromic glass walls were used in the computer centre, from where the entire gas network is controlled; and in the conference areas, there is a flush-glazed façade with blinds.

Aufgrund von hoher Sonnenstrahlung und Wärmegewinn ist die südliche Fassade wesentlich geschlossener als ihr nördliches Gegenstück.

In view of the high degree of insolation and great thermal gains, the south façade is closed over a greater part of its area than the north face.

Auf der südlichen Kathedralwand liegt der Sonnenschutz außen.

The sunshading system to the south cathedral wall is fixed externally.

Die nördliche Kathedralwand kommt ohne Sonnenschutz aus. Der Konferenzturm hat innenliegend Jalousien.

The north cathedral wall requires no sunshading. Internal blinds were installed in the conference tower.

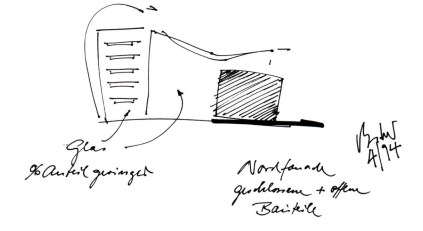

Zur Straße hin prägen doppelte Fassaden die Erscheinung des Gebäudes. Die äußere einfache Verglasung ist geschoßhoch und punktgehalten. Die Halterungen aus glasperlgestrahltem Edelstahl nehmen Toleranzen in jede Richtung auf. Aufgrund thermischer Bedingungen bewegt sich die äußere Fassade allein in der Länge um plus oder minus drei Zentimeter. Die innere Fassade besteht aus Verbund-Sicherheits-Scheiben von 1,5 mal 3,5 Metern. Im Zwischenraum von 25 bis 75 Zentimeter hängen mikroperforierte Jalousien. Die als T ausgeführten Pfosten der äußeren Fassade geben den Lamellen Führung. Unerwünschte Wärmezufuhr durch Sonnenstrahlung an den Stößen der Jalousien wird so vermieden. Aufgrund der Beschichtung der Lamellen reflektiert das Tageslicht bis tief ins Gebäudeinnere. Ihre Perforation diffundiert alle Sonnenstrahlen, erlaubt jedoch auch bei völlig geschlossenen Jalousien eine für die Arbeit am Bildschirm günstige Sicht von innen nach außen.

Along the street, the building is enclosed by double-layer façades. The outer skin of single glazing consists of storey-height point-fixed units. The fixings – in stainless steel with a glass-bead-blasted finish – can absorb movements in all directions. Thermal activity can cause movements over the entire length of the outer skin of up to ± three centimetres. The inner façade layer consists of panes of laminated safety glass 1.5 x 3.5 metres in size. Microperforated blinds are suspended in the 25–75 centimetre intermediate space. The T-section posts of the outer façade layer serve as guide tracks for the blinds. Thereby obviating unwanted heat gains from insolation at the joints between the blinds. The coating to the louvres deflects daylight deep into the interior of the building. The perforations diffuse the direct rays of the sun, but nevertheless allow a view out of the building for staff working on computer monitors, even when the blinds are completely closed.

$k = 1.0\ W/m^2K$
$g = 0.25$
$R_w = 45\ dB$

Details der östlichen Fassade. Die Jalousien im Zwischenraum sind mikroperforiert und low-E-beschichtet.

East façade details. The blinds in the intermediate space are microperforated and low-E coated.

Der Anschluß zwischen beiden Klimafassaden war eine Herausforderung. Thermisch bedingt bewegen sich die inneren und äußeren Fassaden unterschiedlich.

The abutment between the two climate-control façades posed a challenge. Different thermal movements occur in the inner and outer layers.

Horizontalschnitt. Anschluß zwischen tiefer und flacher Klimafassade

1 Silikonprofil
2 Punkthalter Edelstahl
3 ESG Verglasung 12 mm
4 Aluminiumprofil natureloxiert mit Stahlkern
5 Mikroperforierte Jalousie
6 Aluminiumgitterrost natureloxiert 35/100 mm
7 Wärmedämmverglasung 29 mm in Aluminiumprofilen natureloxiert, teilweise Drehflügel
8 Fassadenanschlußschwert
9 Bodenkonvektor
10 GK Ständerwand, streiflichtfrei, gespachtelt und gestrichen

Horizontal section. Abutment between deep and shallow climate-control façades

1 silicone strip
2 stainless-steel point fixings
3 12 mm toughened safety glass
4 natural-anodized aluminium section with steel core
5 microperforated louvre blind
6 natural-anodized aluminium grating (35/100 mm)
7 29 mm low-E glass in natural-anodized aluminium frame; partly as pivoting casement
8 façade fixing plate
9 floor convector
10 plasterboard stud partition, smoothed to avoid highlights and painted

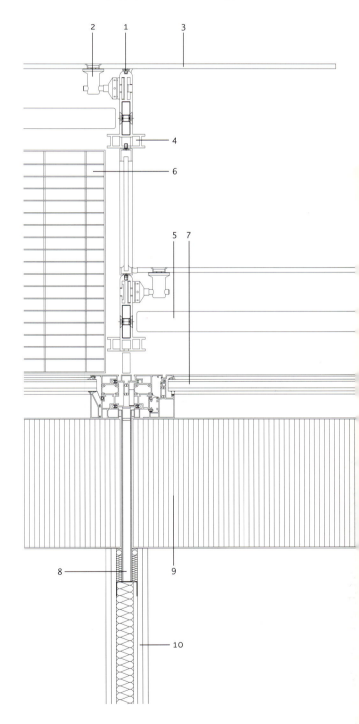

Am Dach kragen die Glasscheiben der äußeren Fassade aus.

The glazing of the outer façade layer projects from the face of the building.

Die gekrümmte Fassade im sechsten Obergeschoß wird von Stahlträgern gehalten. Sie sind wasserdurchströmt.

The curved façade to the sixth floor is fixed to steel supporting members through which water flows.

Zwischenraum der Klimafassade. Die innere doppelte Verglasung ist facettiert, die äußere Scheibe gebogen und an Planarhaltern befestigt.

Intermediate space between the two façade layers. The inner double glazing is facetted; the outer layer is curved and attached to planar fixings.

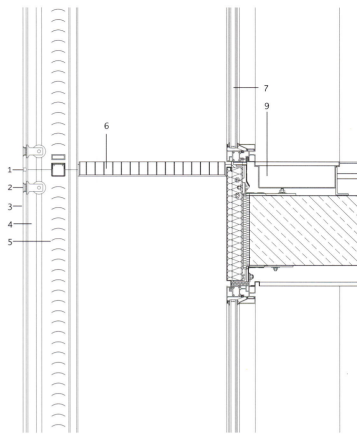

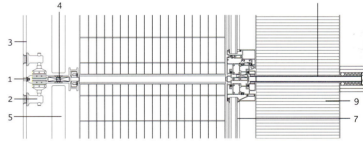

Vertikal- und Horizontalschnitt Klimafassade

1 Silikonprofil
2 Punkthalter Edelstahl
3 ESG Verglasung 12 mm
4 Aluminiumhohlprofil natureloxiert mit Stahlkern
5 Mikroperforierte Jalousie
6 Aluminiumgitterrost natureloxiert 35/100 mm
7 Wärmedämmverglasung 29 mm in Aluminiumprofilen natureloxiert, teilweise Drehflügel
8 Fassadenanschlußschwert
9 Bodenkonvektor

Vertical and horizontal sections through climate-control façade

1 silicone strip
2 stainless-steel point fixings
3 12 mm toughened safety glass
4 natural-anodized aluminium hollow section with steel core
5 microperforated louvre blind
6 natural-anodized aluminium grating (35/100 mm)
7 29 mm low-E glass in natural-anodized aluminium frame; partly as pivoting casement
8 façade fixing plate
9 floor convector

Auf den inneren Fassaden sorgen Lamellen in den Kernbereichen sowie die Perforierung der Brüstungen und Reinigungsbalkone für eine bessere Akustik.

In the core areas, louvres to the inner façades and perforations in the balustrades and maintenance balconies serve to improve the acoustics.

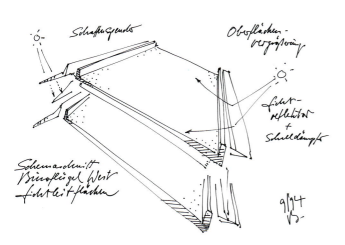

Die beiden Innenfassaden sind als Pfosten-Riegel-Konstruktion ausgeführt. Wegen der klimatischen Konditionen des Atriums blieben die Aluminium-T-Profile ohne thermische Trennung und so besonders schlank. Die Senkklapp-Lüftungs-Fenster lassen sich zum Binnenhof öffnen. Die Reinigungsbalkone sind auf der Unterseite mit Lochblechen verkleidet. Sie schützen vor Blendung und verbessern die Akustik des Atriums.

The two internal façades to the atrium are in a post-and-rail construction. In view of the controlled indoor climate within the atrium, it was possible to design the aluminium T-sections without a thermal division and thus ensure slender dimensions. The top-hung ventilating flaps can be opened to the internal courtyard. The soffits of the maintenance balconies in front of the façades are clad with perforated sheet metal. They protect against glare and also improve the acoustics within the atrium.

$k = 2.25 \text{ W/m}^2\text{K}$
$g = 0.25$
$R_w = 30 \text{ dB}$

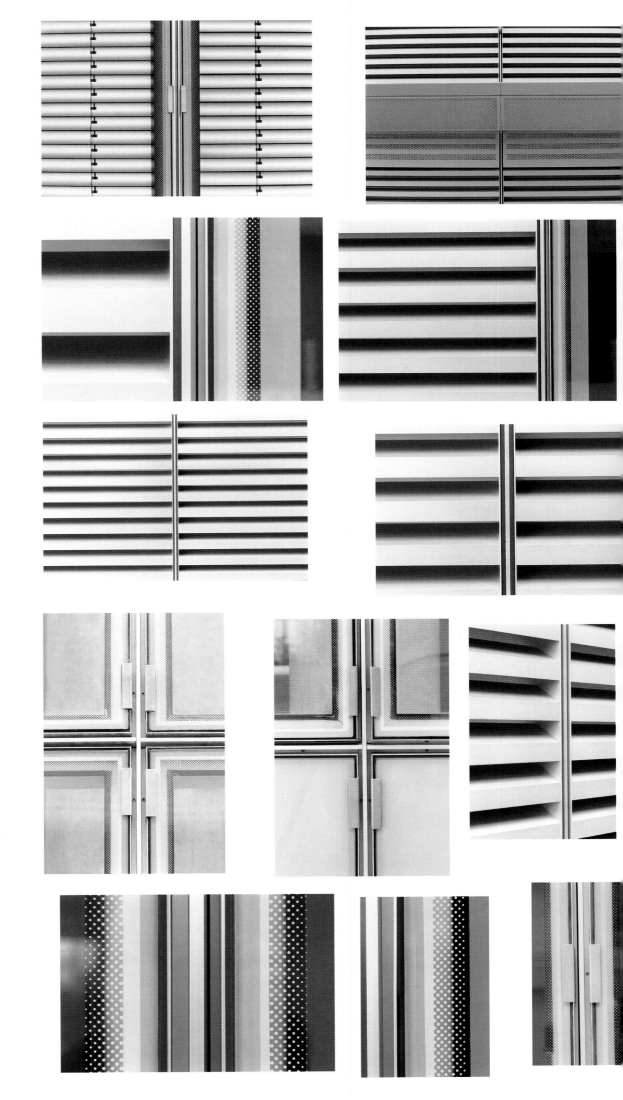

Details der Fassaden im Atrium.

Details of the atrium façades.

Die perforierten Akustiksegel filtern das Sonnenlicht und werfen sanfte Schatten auf die Fenster unter ihnen.

Perforated acoustic "sails" filter the sunlight and cast soft shadows on the windows beneath.

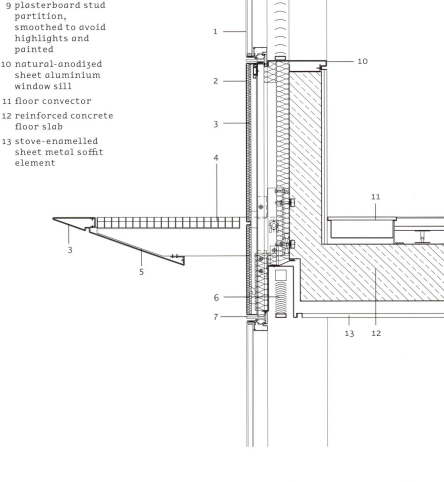

Vertical and horizontal sections through atrium façade

1 top-hung ventilating flap, low-E glass fixed with adhesive and mechanically secured
2 natural-anodized perforated sheet aluminium lined internally with sound-absorbing mineral-wool insulation
3 sheet aluminium cladding
4 natural-anodized aluminium grating (35/100 mm)
5 perforated sheet aluminium
6 perforated internal louvre sunblind
7 aluminium section
8 façade fixing plate
9 plasterboard stud partition, smoothed to avoid highlights and painted
10 natural-anodized sheet aluminium window sill
11 floor convector
12 reinforced concrete floor slab
13 stove-enamelled sheet metal soffit element

Vertikal- und Horizontalschnitt Atriumfassade

1 Senkklapp-Lüftungs-Flügel Wärmeschutzverglasung verklebt und mechanisch gesichert
2 Gelochtes Aluminiumblech natureloxiert, mit schallabsorbierender Mineralwollmatte hinterlegt
3 Aluminiumblech
4 Aluminiumgitterrost 35/100 mm natureloxiert
5 Perforiertes Aluminiumblech
6 Innenliegende Sonnenschutzjalousie perforiert
7 Aluminiumprofil
8 Fassadenanschlußschwert
9 GK-Ständerwand streiflichtfrei gespachtelt und gestrichen
10 Fensterbank, Aluminiumblech natureloxiert
11 Bodenkonvektor
12 Geschoßdecke Stahlbeton
13 Deckenelement Blech einbrennlackiert

Vertikalschnitt und Grundriß der nördlichen Kathedralwand. Die Lüftungsöffnungen werden durch die Gebäudeleittechnik gesteuert.

Vertical and horizontal sections through northern cathedral wall to atrium. The ventilation openings are operated via the control and instrumentation system.

1 Aluminiumfassadenpfosten, natureloxiert mit Stahlkern
2 Verbundsicherheitsverglasung
3 Senkklapp-Lüftungs-Flügel. Verbundsicherheitsglas verklebt und mechanisch gesichert in Aluminiumprofilen, natureloxiert
4 Öffnungsmechanik, druckluftgesteuert

1 natural-anodized aluminium façade post with steel core
2 laminated safety glass
3 top-hung ventilating flap. Laminated safety glass fixed with adhesive and mechanically secured in natural-anodized aluminium frame
4 pneumatically operated opening mechanism

Wegen ihrer Größe und ihres hochragenden Charakters nennen wir die Schmalseiten des Atriums auch Kathedralwände. Hier, an der Nord- und Südseite, bilden abgehängte Pfosten-Riegel-Konstruktionen den Abschluß von Binnenhof und Stufenberg. Der Aussteifung dienen 17,5 Meter lange waagrechte Träger. Die Wärmeschutzverglasung besteht aus Einscheiben-Sicherheitsglas in zwei Schichten. An der nördlichen Fassade sorgen große Senkklapp-Lüftungs-Flügel für frische Luft. Sie werden je nach Wetter durch das digitale Leitsystem geöffnet oder geschlossen. Die Leittechnik steuert auch die außen montierten Jalousien der südlichen Fassade.

We refer to the north and south end faces of the atrium as "cathedral walls" because of their size and lofty character. The internal courtyard space with its cascade of levels is closed here by a suspended post-and-rail construction. Bracing is provided by 17.5-metre horizontal girders. The thermally insulating glazing consists of two layers of toughened safety glass. Large window flaps in the north face allow fresh air to enter this space. Depending on weather conditions, they may be electromechanically opened and closed by the digital control system. The external blinds to the south face are also operated by means of the control and instrumentation technology.

$k = 1.4 \text{ W/m}^2\text{K}$
$g = 0.25$
$Rw = 30 \text{ dB}$

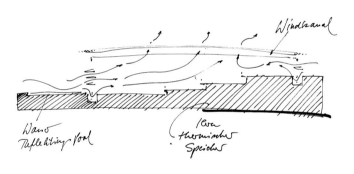

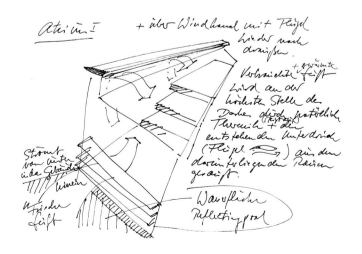

Nördliche Kathedralwand mit windaussteifenden Horizontalträgern und Lüftungsöffnungen vor dem »Reflecting Pool«.

Northern cathedral wall with horizontal wind-bracing members and with ventilation openings. Beyond the wall is the reflecting pool.

Außenliegender feststehender Sonnenschutz über der Konferenzetage des Westflügels.

Fixed external sunshading over the conference level in the western tract.

Zum Garten hin besteht die Fassade aus Structural-Glazing-Fenster-Elementen mit thermisch getrennten Profilen und gedämmter Verkleidung im Bereich der Brüstung. Die Reinigungsbalkone sind Teil der festen, gewinkelten Blendschutzflügel. Die Senkklapp-Lüftungs-Fenster sind zum Öffnen mit verdeckten Bändern versehen, ihre Doppelscheiben in schmale Rahmen geklebt und am Rande bedruckt. Dadurch können die Pfosten schmal bleiben. Der Blendschutz gibt der Fassade eine starke waagrechte, die Pfosten geben ihr eine feine senkrechte Gliederung.

The façade overlooking the garden consists of structural-sealant-glazing elements with thermally divided frames and insulated cladding to the apron walls. The servicing balconies are integrated into the fixed, angled sunscreen elements. The top-hung ventilating window flaps are fitted with concealed hinges. The panes of double glazing are adhesive fixed in narrow frames and have a printed surface at the edges – a feature that allowed the posts to be designed with slender dimensions. The sunscreen installation lends the façade a bold horizontal articulation. The posts, in contrast, form fine vertical divisions.

$k = 1.8\ W/m^2K$
$g = 0.25$
$R_w = 30\ dB$

Vertikal- und Horizontalschnitt Gartenfassade

1. Fensterbank Aluminiumblech, natureloxiert
2. Senkklapp-Lüftungs-Fenster mit Sonnenschutzisolierverglasung in Aluminiumprofile verklebt, Aluminiumprofil natureloxiert
3. Aluminiumblechverkleidung, natureloxiert
4. Aluminiumgitterrost 35/100 mm
5. Sonnenschutzflügel, Aluminium natureloxiert
6. Aluminiumschwert, natureloxiert
7. Innenliegende Sonnenschutzjalousie, Aluminiumlamellen
8. Deckenelement, Blech einbrennlackiert
9. Fassadenanschlußschwert
10. GK-Verkleidung
11. Bodenkonvektor
12. Geschoßdecke Stahlbeton

Vertical and horizontal sections through garden façade

1. natural-anodized sheet aluminium window sill
2. top-hung ventilating flap, low-E glazing fixed with adhesive in natural-anodized aluminium frame
3. natural-anodized sheet aluminium cladding
4. natural-anodized aluminium grating (35/100 mm)
5. natural-anodized aluminium sun-shading element
6. natural-anodized aluminium fixing bracket
7. aluminium louvre internal blind
8. stove-enamelled sheet metal soffit element
9. façade fixing plate
10. plasterboard wall lining
11. floor convector
12. reinforced concrete floor slab

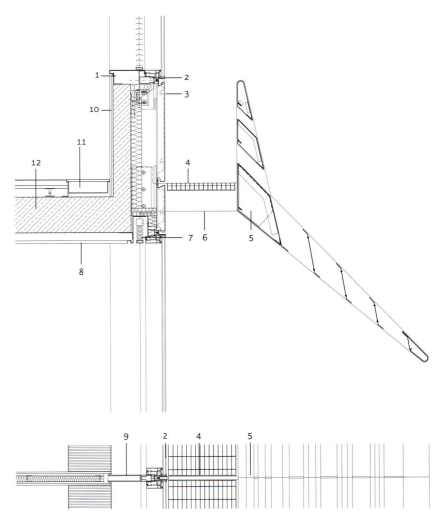

Doer or artist

Macher oder Künstler

Die Position des Architekten verändert sich. Die alte Frage nach dem Macher hier oder dem Künstler dort stellt sich in dieser Form schon lange nicht mehr. Denn die Aufgaben sind so vielfältig geworden, daß heute zu ihrer Lösung Wissen aus den verschiedensten Disziplinen der Technologie wie auch anderer Bereiche notwendig ist. Je stärker sich der Architekt für eine Spezialisierung entscheidet, ob in Richtung Macher oder in Richtung Künstler, je stärker muß er damit rechnen, daß die von ihm nicht gelösten Probleme von anderen gelöst werden. Möchte er jedoch Autorität als Gestalter gewinnen und für den Bauherrn der wichtigste Partner bleiben, so muß er sich über das reine Entwerfen hinaus Kompetenz verschaffen.

In dieser Lage bietet das interdisziplinäre Designteam, mit dem Architekten als Generalisten, einen Ausweg. Für den Bauherrn vereinfacht es die Kommunikation. Statt sich mit verschiedenen Beteiligten verständigen zu müssen, hat er einen verantwortlichen Ansprechpartner. Der Wunsch des Bauherrn nach einem Generalplanervertrag kam unserer Arbeitsweise entgegen. Ohne auf vorherige Verpflichtungen des Bauherrn eingehen zu müssen, konnten wir das Designteam nach rein fachlichen Gesichtspunkten zusammenstellen.

The position of the architect is changing. The old images of the profession – on the one hand, the master builder who gets things done; on the other, the artist – lost their validity long ago, at least in this form. The responsibilities have become so many and varied that specialist knowledge from all fields of technology and from other disciplines is required to tackle a construction project today. The more architects decide to specialize – in the direction of the high-powered professional or that of the artist – the more they will have to rely on others to solve the problems they cannot handle. If architects wish to wield authority as designers and remain the client's most important partner, they must acquire competences that go far beyond the realm of design.

In a situation such as this, the interdisciplinary design team, with the architect as a generalist, offers a viable solution. For one thing, it simplifies the lines of communication for the client. Instead of having to get in touch individually with all the different parties involved in a scheme, he will have a single partner with overall responsibility. In the present case, the developer's wish for a contract with a single general planning team suited our method of work. Without having to take account of prior contractual obligations into which the developer might have entered, we were free to put together a design team on a completely objective basis.

Werner Hauenherm
Werner Keutmann
Walter Weiss
Eike Becker

Staying power

Mit langem Atem

Eike Becker
Werner Keutmann

Eike Becker: Bauherr dieses Neubaus für die Verbundnetz Gas AG war der geschlossene Immobilienfonds Bürohaus Leipzig Nordost GbR, der aus privaten Personen besteht. Vor Ort nehmen Sie bis heute deren Interessen wahr. Was genau tun Sie?

Werner Keutmann: Ich bin Prokurist der Kölner Unternehmensgruppe Esch und entwickle Projekte. In der ersten Phase geht es um die Akquisition eines Grundstücks, dann um die Vorplanung für das Areal, schließlich um den Weg von der Entwurfsplanung bis zur Baugenehmigung. Dabei bedienen wir uns örtlicher Architekten, manchmal auch renommierter Architekturbüros. Der Vertrag mit dem Architekten umfaßt zunächst alle Leistungen bis zur Baureife. In der zweiten Phase geht es um die Errichtung des Objekts, mit der Qualitäts- und Kostenkontrolle. In der dritten Phase geht es um den Nutzer. Wenn sich das Objekt im Rohbau befindet, beginnen wir mit der Verhandlung eines Mietvertrages. Danach begleite ich das Objekt noch bis zur mängelfreien Fertigstellung und zur Übergabe an den Mieter. Erst dann geht der Bau in die Obhut der Oppenheim Vermögens- und Immobilien GmbH über.

Die Josef Esch Fonds Projekt GmbH und die Gebrüder Esch Wohnbaugesellschaft mbH haben während der letzten Jahre einen großen Aufschwung genommen. Sie haben nicht allein dieses Projekt entwickelt, sondern auch die Arena in Köln. Auf der Deutzer Seite entstand nach amerikanischem Konzept ein Komplex für über 18 000 Veranstaltungsbesucher.

Die Unternehmensgruppe Esch hat drei Standbeine. Das erste ist der Wohnungsbau mit etwa 500 Einheiten pro Jahr. Das zweite ist die gewerbliche Immobilie. In der Regel handelt es sich um Bürobauten, zum Beispiel um die Zentrale der e plus Service GmbH in Düsseldorf. Die Untergrenze des Finanzvolumens solcher Objekte liegt bei etwa 50 Millionen Mark, in den meisten Fällen darüber. Das dritte Standbein sind gemischt genutzte Objekte. Sie haben die Köln Arena erwähnt, für uns ein Novum. Für den Bau konnten wir die Architekten Gottfried und Peter Böhm gewinnen. Es ist der größte Komplex dieser Art in Europa, in bezug auf die Nutzung ein Konzept, wie man es bei Hallen in den USA findet. Wir machen da nicht allein Sport und Musik, sondern auch Unterhaltung en gros.

Woher kommt der Erfolg?

Wir haben eine kleine Mannschaft mit persönlicher Verantwortung. Aber wir machen nicht alles selber. Die wichtigste Aufgabe besteht vielmehr darin, hochkompetente, das heißt effiziente und flexible Partner zu finden. Bei der Grundstücksuche kooperieren wir mit großen Maklerbüros. Es geht weiter mit der baulichen Vorplanung durch Architekten. Schon früh treten Ingenieure, Notare und andere Fachleute hinzu. Sehr wichtig ist der Projektsteuerer, der das Vorhaben von Anfang an betreut, auch wenn wir das Objekt später vielleicht fallen lassen. Wir realisieren nur Objekte, von denen wir durch und durch überzeugt sind, bei denen also die planerische, die bauliche und die kaufmännische Seite stimmen. Wo das nicht der Fall ist, brechen wir ab.

Steht hinter Ihrem Erfolg etwa die richtige Mischung aus Sachlichkeit und Wagemut? Ich denke an Ihre Verbindung zum Bankhaus Oppenheim.

Wir sind mit dem Bankhaus Sal. Oppenheim jr. & Cie durch eine Holding verbunden. So unterliegen wir Kontrollen, die bei Banken üblich sind. Jede Planung beginnt mit einer simplen Rechnung. Wir

Eike Becker: The developer of this new building for the Verbundnetz Gas AG was a closed-end property fund: the Bürohaus Leipzig Nordost GbR, an organization consisting of private persons. Even today, you are still looking after their interests on site. What exactly do you do?

Werner Keutmann: I have power of attorney for the Esch business group in Cologne, and it is my responsibility to develop projects. In the first phase of a development, one is concerned with the acquisition of a piece of land, then with the preliminary planning for the site, and finally, with the path that leads from the design planning to the stage of gaining local authority permission for the scheme. For this purpose, we generally use the services of local architects, though on some occasions, we also approach well-known architectural practices. The contract with the architect includes all services up to the completion of the planning. The second phase comprises the erection of the building, with quality and cost controls. The third phase revolves around the user. Once the carcass structure has been completed, we start negotiating the lease. After that, I supervise the progress of the project up to its completion and the remedying of defects, to the point when the building is handed over to the lessee. Only at that point does it pass into the hands of the Oppenheim Vermögens- und Immobilien GmbH.

The Josef Esch Fonds Projekt GmbH and the Gebrüder Esch Wohnbaugesellschaft mbH have both experienced a considerable boom in the past few years. They were responsible not only for the development of this project, but also for the Arena scheme in Cologne. On the Deutz side of the Rhine, a complex for more than 18,000 visitors was created according to an American concept.

The Esch group has three main areas of activity. The first is housing, with about 500 units a year. The second is commercial developments, which, as a rule, mean offices: for example, the headquarters of the e-plus Service GmbH in Düsseldorf. Objects of this kind usually have a minimum budget of around DM 50 million, though in most cases it's higher than that. The third area of activity lies in developments with mixed uses. You mentioned the Cologne Arena project. That was something new for us. We managed to obtain the services of the architects Gottfried and Peter Böhm for that development. It will be the largest complex of its kind in Europe. In terms of its use, it's the sort of concept one finds in the US. We're concerned not only with sport and music here, but with large-scale entertainment as a whole.

To what do you attribute your success?

We have a small team of people who all bear personal responsibility. But we don't do everything ourselves. The most important thing is to find highly competent partners, which means people who are both efficient and flexible. In our search for suitable sites, for example, we collaborate with big property firms. The process continues with the preliminary constructional planning by the architects. Engineers, notaries and other specialists are involved at an early stage, too. One extremely important person is the project manager, who supervises the scheme from the very beginning, even if we may ultimately abandon it. We go ahead with projects only when we are absolutely convinced of them; in other words, where the planning, constructional and commercial aspects are right. Where that's not the case, we simply drop the scheme.

Is it perhaps the right balance of prudence and daring that lies behind your success? I'm thinking of your links to the Oppenheim banking house.

Our links with the Sal. Oppenheim Jr. & Cie. banking house are in the form of a holding. As a result, we are subject to the kind of controls that are customary with banks. Every planning project begins with a simple calculation. We calculate the costs, and from that figure we derive the investment sum required and, in turn, the rental income that will be necessary. We pursue a scheme only if these figures are right. In the early phase of a project, we are not interested in what the development may look like one day or who will use it. The decisive thing is whether the building will prove financially viable.

Among colleagues I often hear complaints about the loss of the client. In contrast to this, my impression of the property fund, in the course of executing the building in Leipzig – and of you in particular – was that you were strong clients.

My function as a developer exists on two levels: as the representative of the investors, and as the person with power of attorney for the Esch group. The role of a client implies leadership, management and exercising control. To guarantee that the cost targets and time schedules are adhered to, I avail myself of the services of a project manager. In Leipzig, it was the office of Prof. Weiss and Partners. I retain the right to overrule all deviations from the work as specified or from agreed samples. Only with this proviso can I prevent the project slipping out of control. It's easy to say I'd like to do this

kalkulieren die Kosten. Daraus folgt eine Investitionssumme und daraus die erforderliche Mieteinnahme. Nur wenn die Zahlen stimmen, bleiben wir bei der Sache. In der frühen Phase eines Projekts interessiert uns nicht, wie das Objekt mal aussieht und wer das Objekt mal benutzt. Ausschlaggebend ist, ob der Bau sich finanziell trägt.

> Unter Kollegen höre ich die Klage über den Verlust des Bauherrn. Im Gegensatz zu dieser Erfahrung habe ich den Immobilienfonds bei der Errichtung des Gebäudes in Leipzig, vor allem Sie selbst, als starken Bauherrn wahrgenommen.

Meine Rolle als Bauherr spielt sich auf zwei Ebenen ab, als Vertreter der Anleger und als Prokurist der Unternehmensgruppe Esch. Bauherrnschaft heißt Leitung, Steuerung, Kontrolle. Um zu gewährleisten, daß der Kosten- und Terminrahmen eingehalten werden, bediene ich mich eines Projektsteuerers, in Leipzig das Büro Prof. Weiss und Partner. Ich behalte mir jede Abweichung vom Bestellwerk und jede Bemusterung vor, da ich nur durch diesen Vorbehalt verhindern kann, daß mir das Projekt entgleitet. Zu sagen, ich möchte dies und das im Neubau lieber anders haben, ist leicht. Auf solche Wünsche kann ich mich aber nur einlassen, wenn sie den Kosten- und Terminrahmen nicht sprengen.

> Manche erleben die Errichtung eines Gebäudes als einen Hürdenlauf, bei dem sie von ihren anfänglichen Vorstellungen immer mehr Abstand nehmen müssen. Was sind die Fehler beim Planen und Bauen?

Diese Enttäuschung läßt sich vermeiden, wenn man als Bauherr das Projekt vom ersten bis zum letzten Moment kontrolliert, wenn man den Rahmen von Geld und Zeit als eine Herausforderung begreift, wenn man das Vertrauen der Anleger als Gebot betrachtet. Sie haben mal gesagt, die Planung sei fertig, wenn der Neubau fertig sei. Diese Offenheit mag für den Architekten sinnvoll sein. Für den Projektentwickler und Projektsteuerer ist sie tödlich. Allerdings müssen wir flexibel bleiben. Man muß Veränderung zulassen und beherrschen. Man muß das Risiko jeder Abweichung vom Bestellwerk, besonders gegenüber dem Generalunternehmer, genau einschätzen.

> Das Gebäude heißt Hauptverwaltung der Verbundnetz Gas AG. Das Unternehmen hatte den Wunsch, daß mit dem Gebäude etwas von seinem Charakter zur Erscheinung kommt, während für die Anleger dieses Bestreben der Benutzer belanglos ist, jedenfalls hinter den ökonomischen Interessen zurücktritt. Welche Probleme folgen daraus?

Sie müssen dem Mieter, falls er sich auf Jahre im Gebäude einrichten möchte, die Möglichkeit geben, seine Identität zu verwirklichen. Dabei gibt es Wünsche ohne Kosten und Wünsche mit Kosten, etwa die Ausstattung mit bestimmten Flurleuchten oder Rolltreppen. In Leipzig mußte dem Neubau ein großes Rechenzentrum integriert werden. Die Kosten solcher Extras werden entweder gleich vom Mieter übernommen oder später durch die Miete abgerechnet. Schwierig wird es nur, wenn der Nutzer auch auf die äußere Gestaltung des Gebäudes Einfluß nehmen will, auf Idee und Konzept der Architektur. Im übrigen planen wir Bürobauten immer so, daß sie von einer Vielzahl von Mietern genutzt werden können. Sie müssen konstruktiv und funktional, ökonomisch und ökologisch sinnvoll sein. Wir orientieren uns immer am guten Standard, würden nie Büroräume mit Übertiefen planen. Heute wird Flexibilität großgeschrieben. Da kommen Sie mit dem Standard weiter als mit der Einzellösung. Wir sitzen hier in einem großen Raum. Ursprünglich sollte er die Bibliothek aufnehmen. Jetzt dient er dem Vorstand für Konferenzen. Und es würde keine Mühe machen, daraus drei Büroräume zu machen. Flexibilität ist ein Merkmal guter Architektur. Ein anderes sind die Details. Ich habe nicht den Eindruck, daß nach der Vergabe der Ausführung an den Generalunternehmer einfachere Lösungen eine Chance hatten. Ich glaube vielmehr, daß die Details durch die häufige Bemusterung besser wurden.

Wenn wir einen Auftrag an einen Generalunternehmer vergeben, dann gehört dazu neben einer genauen Beschreibung des Gebäudes die Vorgabe von 300 bis 400 Details. Dieses Paket muß so viel Spielraum haben, daß jede Einzellösung, etwa die Fußböden oder die Geländer, noch verändert werden kann. Aus diesem Grunde darf man den Mindestanspruch auf Nutzbarkeit und Gestaltung nie zu niedrig ansetzen. Es reicht auch nicht, daß hier und dort ein Detail gelungen ist. Es kommt auf die Stimmigkeit im Gesamten an. Manche Leute glauben, mit einer Wohnung voller moderner Klassiker habe man ein ästhetisches Interieur. Dann steht der Corbusier neben dem Mackintosh. Jeder für sich ist gut. Aber es fehlt die Stimmigkeit.

> Und morgen? Wie wird das Bauen in Zukunft sein?

Ich habe meine Befürchtungen. Unter dem wachsenden Kostendruck werden wir immer seltener in der Lage sein, Bauten mit hohem Anspruch zu verwirklichen. Wo man später nur eine Miete von 20 Mark pro Quadratmeter erzielen kann, hat man einen so engen Rahmen, daß bestimmte bauliche Maßnahmen gar nicht mehr in Frage kommen. Ich weiß, daß gute Architektur nicht unbedingt an viel Geld gebunden ist. Aber Qualität und Innovation haben ihren Preis. Wer als Bauherr Neues wagen möchte, muß einen langen Atem haben.

or that differently in a new construction scheme. I can agree to wishes of that kind only if they don't burst the budget and upset the time schedule.

> Some people regard the erection of a building as a handicap race, in the course of which they are forced to diverge further and further from their initial concepts. What mistakes are made in the process of planning and building?

Disappointments can be avoided if you, as the client, have the project under control from the very beginning to the very end; if you understand the cost and time limits as a challenge; and if you regard the trust of your investors as an obligation. You once said that the planning is finished when the building is finished. This open attitude may be meaningful for an architect; but for the developer and the project manager it is fatal. Admittedly, one has to be flexible. One has to be able to accept and control change, and to assess precisely the risk of every deviation from the work as specified, especially from the point of view of the main contractor.

> The building is known as the headquarters of the Verbundnetz Gas AG. The concern wished the structure to express something of its corporate character. For the investors, on the other hand, users' wishes of this kind are of no interest; or at least, they take a back seat to the economic interests. What problems arise from this?

If a tenant intends to occupy a building for many years to come, you have to give him the opportunity to express his identity. There are, of course, wishes that cost nothing and wishes that cost a lot of money: the installation of escalators or special corridor lights, for example. In Leipzig, a large computer centre had to be integrated into the building. The costs of extras of this kind are either borne directly by the tenant, or they have to be accounted for later in the rent.

> Difficulties arise when the user wishes to have a say in the external design of a building – to influence the idea and concept of the architecture. Normally, we plan office blocks in such a way that they can be used by a variety of tenants. They have to make sense structurally and functionally, economically and ecologically. Our aim is always to provide a good standard. We would never plan office spaces with excessive depths, for example. Flexibility is the big thing today. In that respect, you can achieve more by complying with standards than by seeking individual solutions. We are sitting in a large space here. Originally, it was meant to house the library. Now it's used by the board for conference purposes; and it would be no great problem to turn it into three offices.

> Flexibility is a sign of good architecture. Another is the detailing. I don't have the impression that, after granting the contract for the execution of the works to a main contractor, simpler solutions would have had much chance. I have a feeling that the details were improved as a result of the frequent checks.

When we grant a contract to a main contractor, the documents include a precise description of the building plus the specification of 300 to 400 details. This package has to allow sufficient latitude for all the individual design solutions – the details for the floors or the handrails, for example – to be changed. For that reason, the minimum functional and design requirements should never be set too low. It's not enough that a few details are successfully resolved here and there. What's important is an overall coherence. Some people believe that a dwelling full of modern classics makes a comfortable, aesthetic interior. The Le Corbusier stands alongside the Mackintosh. Each may be good in its own right, but a sense of harmony is lacking.

> And in the future? What will construction be like tomorrow?

I have my fears. Faced with increasing cost pressures, we shall be less and less in a position to create buildings of a high standard. Where a rent of only DM 20 per square metre can be obtained in the future, the constraints are so tight that certain constructional measures will no longer be possible. I know that good architecture does not automatically cost a lot of money, but quality and innovation have their price. A developer who wants to try something new will have to have a lot of staying power.

All totally different

Alles völlig anders

Werner Hauenherm

Eike Becker: Der »Volkseigene Betrieb Verbundnetz Gas« wurde von der Treuhandanstalt schon im Sommer 1990 in eine Aktiengesellschaft umgewandelt. Allein das war für Ihr Unternehmen sicher ein starker Einschnitt. Doch damit nicht genug, haben Sie bereits zwei Jahre später angefangen zu überlegen, mit der gesamten Verwaltung auf ein anderes Gelände und in ein anderes Gebäude zu ziehen. Welche Gründe gab es dafür?

Werner Hauenherm: Bis zu unserem Einzug in den Neubau saß die Firma im Kreis Leipzig Land. Wir arbeiteten in Böhlitz-Ehrenberg, in acht mit der Zeit sehr schäbig gewordenen Bauten. Um marktfähig zu werden und im Wettbewerb bestehen zu können, mußte die Verbundnetz Gas AG mächtig aufholen. Wir mußten die Gas-Steuerungs-Systeme erneuern und erweitern, was in den bis dahin benutzten Gebäuden wirtschaftlich unmöglich war. Und wir wollten aus dem Kreis in die Stadt. Bei der Suche nach Partnern stießen wir dann auf die Josef Esch Fonds Projekt GmbH, die schon über ein Grundstück in einem Leipziger Gewerbegelände verfügte und dort den Neubau eines Bürohauses plante.

Die Aussicht auf einen neuen Ort und einen neuen Bau, das muß doch bei den Angestellten für Gespräche gesorgt haben. Wie haben Sie die Mitarbeiter einbezogen?

Der Umzug an sich wurde allgemein begrüßt. In ein und demselben Gebäude ist die Kommunikation viel leichter als in acht verschiedenen Bauten. Der Entwurf aber, die Skizzen und das Modell aus Ihrem Büro, das war für uns alle eine echte Überraschung. Sie können sich denken, daß es angesichts der für die Belegschaft ungewöhnlichen Modernität des geplanten Bürohauses geteilte Meinungen gab. Manche waren stolz auf diese Zukunft. Manche wünschten sich mehr Farbe, manche auch mehr Gemütlichkeit.

Ein Unternehmen wie die Verbundnetz Gas AG baut nicht alle Tage. Viele Nutzer finden es schwer, ihre Interessen zu formulieren. Wie haben Sie sich sprachfähig gemacht? Was haben Sie getan, damit Ihre Wünsche in bezug auf das Gebäude in Erfüllung gingen?

Unter Einbeziehung der Fachbereiche und des Betriebsrates haben wir unter meiner Leitung ein Team gebildet, das die Forderungen des Unternehmens in bezug auf den Neubau genau analysiert hat. Wir hatten, vertraglich gesichert, ein allgemeines Mitspracherecht bei der Gestaltung und Ausführung. Ferner gab es Mietersonderwünsche, die der Bauherr weitgehend verwirklicht hat. Das meiste im Verhältnis zwischen den Beteiligten war juristisch präzise definiert. Aber das wichtigste war die ständige Bereitschaft, divergente Positionen in einen Konsens fließen zu lassen. Erinnern Sie sich noch an die zahllosen Jours Fixes und Policy Meetings, bei denen Professor Weiss die Rolle des Vermittlers spielte?

Natürlich. Aber ich drehe die Frage mal um. Haben Sie aus dem ganzen Prozeß noch eine Schlüsselszene im Kopf?

Ich erinnere mich gut an den ersten Anruf in Ihrem Architekturbüro. Ich glaube, es war ein Freitagmittag. Bei Ihnen war schon keiner mehr da. So mußte ich meine Glückwünsche zum großen Auftrag auf Band sprechen. Lange nach meinem ersten Besuch in Ihrem Büro vertrauten Sie mir an, daß Sie zu dieser Gelegenheit ein paar Studenten angeheuert hatten, um einen guten Eindruck zu machen. Es mußte wohl alles etwas besser und größer aussehen, weil viele Bauherren jungen und kleinen Büros eine Aufgabe von der Art wie unser Leipziger Gebäude nicht zutrauen. Was für unser Unternehmen nicht leicht war, war die

Eike Becker: In the summer of 1990, the Volkseigener Betrieb Verbundnetz Gas, a state-owned gas supply concern, was transformed into a joint-stock company by the Treuhandanstalt [the German state organization responsible for the privatization of business enterprises in what was formerly East Germany]. That in itself was certainly a momentous turning point for your organization. As if that were not enough, though, only two years later you started thinking of moving the entire administration to another building in another location. What were the reasons for that?

Werner Hauenherm: Up to the time we moved into the new building, the company had its seat in the rural district of Leipzig. Our work was carried out in Böhlitz-Ehrenberg in eight buildings that had become rather dilapidated in the course of time. To make itself a competitive organization capable of surviving on the open market, the Verbundnetz Gas AG had to make up an enormous amount of ground. We had to renew and extend the gas control systems – something that would have been economically impossible in the buildings we had been using up to that time. We also wanted to move from the periphery into the city centre. In our search for partners, we came across the Josef Esch Fonds Projekt GmbH, which had a site in a commercial area in Leipzig and was planning a new office development there.

The prospect of moving into a new building in a new location must have sparked off quite a discussion among the employees. How did you involve the staff in this process?

The move in itself was generally welcomed. Communication is much simpler when everyone is working in the same house instead of being scattered over eight different buildings. The design, however – the sketches and the model your office made – was a genuine surprise for all of us. You can imagine that opinions were divided, in view of the exceptional modernity of the proposed office building in the eyes of the staff. Some were proud of the future it represented. Some wanted more colour. Others wanted a cosier atmosphere...

A company like the Verbundnetz Gas AG doesn't build every day. For a lot of users, it's not easy to formulate their needs and interests. How did you find a means of expressing these things? What did you do to make sure that your wishes, in respect of the building, were met?

We drew the various specialist departments and the staff council into the discussions and formed a team – headed by me – that made a close analysis of the company's requirements in terms of the new headquarters. We were guaranteed, by contract, a say in the design and execution of the building. We, as tenants, also had special wishes, which the developer implemented to a large extent. Most aspects of the relations between the various parties were precisely defined by contract. The most important thing, though, was the constant readiness to seek consensus when divergent positions arose. Do you remember all the regular conferences and policy meetings at which Professor Weiss played a mediating role?

Yes, of course. But let me return the question. Is there a key scene from this whole process that comes to mind for you?

I vividly recall the first time I phoned your practice. It was a Friday lunchtime, I think. There was no one left in your office. I had to express my congratulations to you on being awarded such a major contract on tape. A long time after my first visit to your office, you confided to me that you had hired a number of students for the occasion, just to make a good impression. It all had to look a bit bigger and better, simply because a lot of clients would not have entrusted a small, young office with an assignment like our Leipzig building. What was not easy for our company was the division of competence between the architects and

Verteilung der Kompetenz zwischen Architekt und Ingenieur. Aus meiner Arbeit weiß ich, daß etwa eine Rohrleitung von Anfang bis Ende, von der ersten Konzeption bis zur letzten Kontrolle, in der Hand eines Ingenieurs liegt. Wir merkten jedoch bald, daß diese berufliche Erfahrung auf das bauliche Vorhaben, das heißt auf ein Projekt mit dem Konflikt zwischen künstlerischem Anspruch und wirtschaftlicher Lösung, nicht übertragbar war. Aber zum Glück hatten wir mit Professor Weiss ja einen erfahrenen Vermittler.

Gibt es Entscheidungen, die Sie heute anders treffen würden?

Bei den Sicherheitsmaßnahmen würden wir heute wohl keinen so hohen Aufwand mehr betreiben. Aber zu Beginn der neunziger Jahre hielt man diese Kontrolltechnik für notwendig. Man wollte das Gebäude und seine inneren Anlagen vor jedweder Art von Anschlägen schützen.

Sie haben zu Beginn gesagt, die Verbundnetz Gas AG habe in bezug auf ihre Technologie mächtig aufholen müssen. Wie steht es nun, auf dem neuen Gelände und in dem neuen Gebäude, mit der Kommunikation?

Man muß unterscheiden zwischen der Wirkung nach außen und der nach innen. Nach außen haben wir ein kleines Problem. Obwohl das Gebäude völlig frei von den üblichen Accessoires der Repräsentation ist, obwohl es also auch beim Vorstand keine Marmorwände und keine Messingschilder gibt, stellt der Neubau für manche einen Luxus dar, was er in Wahrheit nicht ist. Anders gesagt, wir fühlen uns mitunter genötigt, diesem oder jenem Kunden freundlich zu erklären, daß das Haus längst nicht so teuer war, wie es auf den ersten Blick scheint. Nach innen ist es wie mit jeder neuen, alltäglichen Annehmlichkeit. Man hält sie bald für selbstverständlich. Wir freuen uns, daß wir hier wohnen. Ja, manchmal sind wir auch stolz. Der Neubau trägt zum Selbstbewußtsein des Unternehmens bei.

Und was ist mit den Arbeitsplätzen?

Was die Ausstattung mit Tischen und Stühlen und Schränken angeht, bieten die Büros einen guten Standard. Was Licht und Luft, Heizung und Kühlung angeht, bieten sie weit mehr. Das persönliche Wohlbefinden der Mitarbeiter am Schreibtisch, vor dem Bildschirm und wo immer sonst im Haus war uns wichtig. Ich möchte aber nicht verhehlen, daß unsere Angestellten mit den technologischen Installationen, obwohl ihre Bedienung von der Schalttafel im Türrahmen doch denkbar einfach ist, anfänglich allerhand Schwierigkeiten hatten. Mit der Zeit spielt sich das wohl ein. Sicher müssen wir noch etwas tun, um die gesamte Anlage wirklich voll zu nutzen. Da lassen sich noch manche Kosten sparen.

Bei der Arbeit gibt es neben der formellen immer auch die informelle Kommunikation, neben den festgelegten Besprechungen immer auch die zufälligen Begegnungen. Spielt das eine Rolle im neuen Haus?

Als wir uns nach dem Umzug plötzlich alle in ein und demselben Gebäude wiederfanden, merkten wir, daß wir uns in den getrennten Häusern am alten Ort auseinandergelebt hatten. Hier ist das völlig anders. Man sieht sich, man trifft sich, im Atrium oder in der Cafeteria. An jedem Werktag werden dort etwa 300 Mittagessen eingenommen. Der große Lichthof schafft eine entspannende und anregende Atmosphäre, wo manches leichter geklärt werden kann als bei einem Termin. Wir haben dort auch Treffen mit Kunden veranstaltet und schon Feste gefeiert. Und vor allem: Wir wollen dort Silvester 1999 mit allen Mitarbeitern das nächste Jahrhundert begrüßen.

the engineers. From my own work, I know that a pipeline, for instance, is in the hands of an engineer from beginning to end, from the initial concept to the final controls. We soon realized that this piece of professional experience was not applicable to the process of construction – in other words, to a project where there is a certain conflict between artistic goals and economic solutions. Fortunately, we had an experienced mediator in the person of Professor Weiss.

> Were there things you would decide differently today?

We certainly wouldn't invest as much in elaborate security measures today. But at the beginning of the 1990s, that kind of control technology was regarded as necessary. We wanted to protect the building and its internal installations against all kinds of attack.

> You said at the beginning that the Verbundnetz Gas AG had a lot of ground to make up in the realm of technology. What's the position today in terms of communication in your new location and your new building?

One has to distinguish between internal and external effects. Outwardly, we have a minor problem. Although the building exhibits none of the usual tokens of prestige, although there are no marble walls, for example, on the executive level and no brass nameplates, the new building is a luxury in the eyes of some people – though, in truth, it's not a luxury at all. In other words, we feel obliged to explain to some customers in a friendly way that the building was by no means as expensive as it may seem at first. Internally, it's the same as with all new, everyday amenities. They are soon taken for granted. We are pleased to have our home here. Sometimes we even feel a sense of pride. The new building helps to bolster the confidence of the concern.

> And what about the workplaces?

As far as the furnishings are concerned – the tables, chairs and cupboards – the offices provide a good standard. As far as light and air, heating and cooling are concerned, they provide much more. The personal well-being of the members of the staff – sitting at their desks, at their computers, or wherever else they may be in the building – was important to us. I don't want to ignore the fact, however, that our employees initially had all sorts of difficulties with the technology, although it is extremely simple to operate by means of the control panels in the door frames. In the course of time, those problems resolved themselves. There are still things we have to do to take full advantage of the plant and installations, and there are still cost savings that could be made.

> People communicate on an informal and a formal level in the course of their work. As well as scheduled meetings, there are always chance encounters. Do these things play a role in the new building?

When we were all suddenly brought together in the same building after our move, we became aware that we had grown apart in the separate blocks of our former location. Things are completely different here. People see each other; they bump into each other in the atrium or the cafeteria. Roughly 300 people lunch there every workday. The large covered courtyard space provides a relaxed and stimulating atmosphere, where certain things can be resolved more easily than in a formal setting. We have organized meetings with clients and held celebrations in the atrium. Most important of all, we want to welcome in the new century there with all our staff on New Year's Eve 1999.

Das Rechenzentrum liegt in der Mitte des Hauses. Dort wird die Gasversorgung der östlichen Bundesländer gesteuert.

The computer centre is situated in the middle of the building. The gas supply for the eastern federal states is regulated there.

Carrot, stick & talks

Zucker, Peitsche & Jour fixe

Walter Weiss

Das Wort »Projekt« leitet sich aus dem lateinischen »proicere« ab; auf deutsch meint es »vorwärtswerfen«, also mit Kraft und Schwung etwas nach vorne bewegen. Am Projekt der Hauptverwaltung für die Verbundnetz Gas AG Leipzig waren im wesentlichen fünf Parteien beteiligt: als Bauherr der Immobilienfonds Bürohaus Leipzig Nordost GbR, vertreten durch die Josef Esch Fonds Projekt GmbH; als Generalplaner Becker Gewers Kühn & Kühn Architekten; als Generalübernehmer die Gebrüder Esch Wohnbaugesellschaft mbH; als Generalunternehmer die Dyckerhoff & Widmann AG; als Nutzer die Verbundnetz Gas AG.

Aufgabe des Projektsteuerers ist es, dafür Sorge zu tragen, daß die voneinander verschiedenen Interessen zu einem optimalen Gesamtwerk geführt werden. Auf der einen Seite ist er, als Auftragnehmer des Bauherrn, selber Partei; auf der anderen Seite muß er sich darum bemühen, daß die Interessen der übrigen Parteien richtig zur Geltung kommen und daß die zahlreichen Schnittstellen differenter Interessen sowie die daraus folgenden Probleme erkannt und gelöst werden. Neben den rein technischen Leistungen muß der Projektsteuerer immer wieder als Mediator, ja als Psychologe wirken. Er muß die Fähigkeiten der Beteiligten richtig einschätzen und unter ihnen, auch durch das eigene Engagement und die eigene Disziplin, eine Atmosphäre schaffen, die jeden anspornt. Nicht selten muß er nach dem Prinzip von Zucker und Peitsche arbeiten, darf sich dabei jedoch nie von seiner professionellen Integrität entfernen.

Damit ein so großes Projekt wie das in Leipzig gelingt, muß die Struktur seiner Organisation vertraglich sorgfältig abgebildet sein. In bezug auf den Neubau des Bürohauses im Gewerbepark Nordost wurde das Aufsetzen und Aushandeln der Verträge für jede einzelne Partei durch eine vom Bauherrn beauftragte Kanzlei besorgt, deren Anwälte das Projekt auch später bei allen Rechtsfragen begleiteten. Gegenstand der Verträge mit den Beteiligten waren nicht allein die Zuständigkeiten und Verantwortungen, sondern auch die wesentlichen Teile des Verfahrens, etwa der Arbeitsablauf oder die Terminpläne oder die Rechnungslegung. Nur so gab es die Sicherheit, daß sich die Parteien strikt an das Vereinbarte hielten.

Auch die Kommunikation der an einem Projekt beteiligten Gruppen bedarf einer präzisen Struktur. Meinungen müssen besprochen, Standpunkte bewertet, Ergebnisse verabschiedet werden. Jede Information von Seiten des Bauherrn oder des Benutzers an die für die Planung und die Ausführung Zuständigen mußte die Projektsteuerung passieren. Anweisungen auf Nebenwegen durfte es auf keinen Fall geben; darum erhielt der Projektsteuerer von jedem Dokument, das zwischen den Parteien ausgetauscht wurde, einen Durchschlag. Erst dieser ständige und genaue Überblick machte es möglich, Probleme zu umgehen, bevor sie überhaupt entstehen konnten.

Um die Kommunikation zu strukturieren, wurden fünf Terminarten geschaffen.

Beim Policy Meeting wurde im Abstand von zwei Monaten die Politik des Projektes auf höchster Ebene festgelegt. An den Policy Meetings nahmen die entscheidungsbefugten Vertreter des Bauherrn, des Mieters und des Generalplaners teil. Auf diesen vom Projektsteuerer geleiteten Treffen wurden auch solche Probleme diskutiert, die die Parteien auf unteren Ebenen nicht hatten lösen können.

The word "project" comes from the Latin verb proicere, which means to "throw something forward"; in other words, to move a thing vigorously ahead. Five main parties were responsible for the new headquarters project for the Verbundnetz Gas AG in Leipzig: the developer (the Immobilienfonds Bürohaus Leipzig Nordost GbR represented by the Josef Esch Fonds Projekt GmbH); the general planner (the architects Becker Gewers Kühn & Kühn); the general assignee (the Esch Wohnbaugesellschaft mbH); the main contractor (Dyckerhoff & Widmann AG); and the user (the Verbundnetz Gas AG).

It is the role of the project manager to ensure that all these different interests are co-ordinated to create an optimum overall development. On the one hand, as the agent of the developer, the project manager represents one of the parties involved. At the same time, he has to ensure that the interests of the other parties are properly represented and that the interfaces between the various interests and the problems arising from these are recognized and resolved. As well as supervising the purely technical aspects, the project manager is repeatedly called upon to act as a mediator, for which a healthy portion of psychology is necessary. He must be able to make a reliable assessment of the various parties and create an atmosphere between them – partly through his own commitment and discipline – that acts as a spur for everyone. On occasion, he will have to use the carrot and stick approach, but he should never lose sight of his professional integrity.

In order to bring a major project like the one in Leipzig to a successful conclusion, the structure of the project manager's organization must be carefully defined by contract. For the office development in the North-East Commercial Park, the contracts with the individual parties were drawn up and negotiated by a lawyers' office appointed by the developer. The lawyers also attended to all legal matters arising subsequently during the course of the scheme. The contracts between the various parties covered not only questions of competence and responsibility. They also set out major elements of the construction process, such as the sequence of work, time scheduling, the rendering of accounts, etc. This was the only way to ensure that the parties adhered strictly to the agreed terms.

Communication between the various groups in a project like this also requires a precisely defined structure. Different opinions have to be discussed, views assessed and decisions reached. Each instruction or piece of information issued by the developer or the user to the parties responsible for the planning and execution of the work had to be vetted by the project manager. Under no circumstances were instructions to bypass his office. For that reason, the project manager received a copy of every document passing between the parties. Only through a process of constant, close supervision like this can problems be nipped in the bud.

In order to create a structure for communication, five different categories of meetings were established.

Every two months, top-level policy meetings were held to determine the general course of the project. These meetings were attended by representatives of the developer, the lessee and the overall planning team, all of whom were invested with decision-making powers. At the policy meetings, which were chaired by the project manager,

Beim Bau-Jour-Fixe mit dem Mieter und beim Bau-Jour-Fixe mit dem Generalunternehmer wurden die akuten Probleme aus der Sicht des Nutzers beziehungsweise des Generalunternehmers besprochen. Ziel der vom Projektsteuerer geleiteten Treffen war die Einigung zwischen den streitenden Parteien. Die Bau-Jours-Fixes fanden alle zwei Wochen statt, in kritischen Phasen des Projekts aber jede Woche.

Auf der Planungsbesprechung wurden von Seiten des Generalunternehmers fast Woche für Woche eher konkrete technische Probleme vorgetragen. In Fällen, wo die Parteien sich nicht einigen konnten, wurde das Problem auf höherer Ebene verhandelt.

Auf der Planungskoordinierungsbesprechung hingegen ging es um Probleme zwischen Generalplaner und Generalunternehmer. Denn im Zuge der Planprüfung durch den Generalplaner trug der Generalunternehmer immer wieder vor, daß zahlreiche Prüfeinträge mit dem Bestellwerk nicht übereinstimmten. Unter Leitung des Projektsteuerers nahmen an diesen Treffen im Abstand von zwei Wochen nicht allein Vertreter des Generalplaners und des Generalunternehmers, sondern auch eine Vielzahl beratender Fachleute aus den Stäben beider Parteien teil. Zusammen mit dem Bauherrn und im Einvernehmen mit den beiden Seiten traf der Projektsteuerer dann Punkt für Punkt eine Entscheidung.

Das wichtigste praktische Instrument zur täglichen Verständigung und Einvernahme unter den Parteien war die Entscheidungsvorlage. Das Projekt selbst wurde durch Wort und Plan in den Verträgen beschrieben. Jede noch so kleine Veränderung an dieser Unterlage, gleich ob in bezug auf den Entwurf oder auf Material und Konstruktion oder auf finanzielle und terminliche Aspekte, durfte erst wirksam werden, wenn der Bauherr eine entsprechende Entscheidungsvorlage unterzeichnet hatte. Dieses standardisierte Dokument mußte der Veranlasser der Veränderung erstellen, mit allen Parteien abstimmen und über den Projektsteuerer dem Bauherrn zur Freigabe einreichen. Dabei bestand für die Beteiligten Bring- und Holschuld. Wenn also eine Seite von irgendeiner Änderung ohne Vorlage Kenntnis hatte, mußte sie dies sofort dem Projektsteuerer mitteilen, der dann die ändernde Partei um eine Vorlage bat.

So stark formalisiert das Verfahren auch wirkt, so sehr trägt es dazu bei, daß alle Parteien zu jeder Zeit über jeden Aspekt des Projekts informiert sind. Die Arbeit mit der Entscheidungsvorlage stärkt außerdem Disziplin und Effizienz. Erstens hält sie Änderungsbegehren an sich im Zaum; zweitens sehen sich die Parteien schon im Vorfeld mit den Konsequenzen ihrer Wünsche konfrontiert; drittens kommt es rascher zur Entscheidung, da das Tankschiff Neubau seinen Kurs erst korrigiert, wenn der Bauherr der Änderung zugestimmt hat.

Während der Planung, das heißt bis zum Abschluß des Vertrags mit dem Generalunternehmer, wurden etwa 750 Entscheidungsvorlagen verabschiedet; während der Ausführung des Gebäudes kamen etwa 700 solcher Dokumente hinzu.

Die Projektkosten wurden schon in einer frühen Phase nach der Elementenmethode genau ermittelt. Das gesamte Vorhaben durchlief dann mehrere Stadien der Einsparung. Zunächst wurde das Gebäude um einige Achsen verkürzt; die Haustechnik wurde vereinfacht. Aufgrund der langwierigen Verhandlungen mit dem Generalunternehmer konnten weitere erhebliche Einsparungen erreicht werden. Der Bauherr verlangte die strikte Einhaltung der Baukosten. Während der Bauzeit traten einige Leistungen hinzu, die jedoch weit unter zwei Prozent der veranschlagten Bausumme von 122 Millionen DM lagen.

Trotz aller manchmal auch harten Auseinandersetzung blieb das Vertrauensverhältnis zwischen den fünf Parteien gewahrt. Was immer in Leipzig geschah, es war geprägt von der Erkenntnis: Wenn wir Probleme haben, dann reden wir miteinander. Und wir versuchen, sie gemeinsam zu lösen.

Walter Weiss

problems were also discussed that the parties had not been able to resolve at a lower level.

The regular constructional meetings with the lessee and with the main contractor were used to discuss acute problems that existed from the point of view of these two parties respectively. The purpose of these meetings, which were also chaired by the project manager, was to reach agreement between the disputing parties. These constructional conferences took place every two weeks. At critical stages of the project, they were held every week.

At the weekly planning conferences, questions of a more concrete technical nature would be raised by the main contractor. In those cases where the parties were unable to agree, the problems would be referred to a higher level for negotiation.

The planning co-ordination meetings, in contrast, dealt with problems arising between the planning team and the main contractor. In the course of checking the plans by engineers, construction firms and others, the planners would make certain amendments, and the general contractor would often remark that these did not correspond with the work as specified and for which he had tendered. In addition to representatives of the general planning team and the main contractor, a number of specialist consultants from the teams of both parties participated in these discussions, which were held every two weeks under the chairmanship of the project manager. Together with the developer, and with the consent of the two sides, the project manager would then decide on each individual issue.

The most important practical instrument for day-to-day communication and agreement between the contracting parties was the variation order. The scope of the project was defined by means of plans and written specifications described in the contract documents. Any variation to these, however small, whether it affected the design, the materials, the form of construction, financial aspects or the time-schedules, could not take effect before the developer had signed the appropriate authorization form. This standard document had to be completed by the party requesting the variation, agreed with all the other parties and then submitted via the project manager for the developer to give his authorization. In this way the various parties were subject to a system that imposed a mutual obligation. In other words, if one party were aware of an unauthorized modification, it would be his duty to report it immediately to the project manager, who would then request the other party to submit a variation form.

However formal this procedure may seem, it helps to ensure that all parties are informed at all times about every aspect of the project. Working with the variation order also strengthens discipline and efficiency. It restrains the urge to make alterations. The parties are confronted in advance with the consequences of their wishes. Decisions are reached more quickly, since the project changes course only when the developer approves of the alterations.

During the planning process – up to the signing of the contract with the main contractor – some 750 variation forms were processed. During the execution of the works, 700 further documents of this kind were submitted.

The costs of the project were precisely calculated at an early stage on a unit estimating basis. The entire development was then subjected to a series of cost-saving measures: the building was reduced in size by a number of bays; the mechanical services were simplified; and protracted negotiations with the main contractor resulted in considerable further savings. The developer insisted on a strict adherence to the contract costs. During the construction phase a number of additional works were required. These remained well below two per cent of the estimated costs of DM 122 million, however.

In spite of all the disputes, some of which were quite heated, the basis of trust between the five parties remained unbroken. Whatever the outcome in Leipzig, the scheme was influenced by the insight that if problems arise, the best thing is to talk to each other and attempt to solve them on a mutual basis.

Walter Weiss

Light art light

Licht Kunst Licht

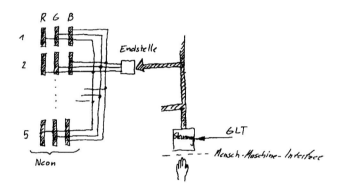

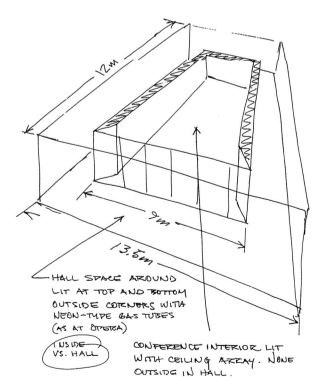

Unsere Vorliebe für die Synästhesie des Barock ließ uns von Beginn der Arbeit an darüber nachdenken, in welcher Weise Künstler am neuen Gebäude der Verbundnetz Gas AG beteiligt werden könnten. Wir dachten dabei nicht an Kunst am Bau. Wir wollen kein Relief an der Wand und keine Plastik vor der Tür. Statt des üblichen Nebeneinanders wollen wir die komplexe Integration des einen im andern, ja die Verschmelzung von Kunst und Bau zu einem neuen Ganzen. Um für einen beschränkten Wettbewerb eine Reihe von Künstlern zu gewinnen, wandten wir uns an den Düsseldorfer Art Consultant Helge Achenbach. Am Wettbewerb nahmen schließlich teil: Dieter Jung aus Berlin, Stephan Jung aus Berlin, Joseph Kossuth aus New York, Jana Milev aus Berlin, Ulf Puder aus Leipzig, George Sexton aus Washington D.C. und James Turrell aus Flagstaff, Arizona.

Die Wahl fiel auf Turrell, bekannt durch seine jahrelange Auseinandersetzung mit Raum und Licht, mit Transparenz und Transluzenz, etwa in seinen »projection pieces« oder seinen »skyspaces«. Schon beim ersten Treffen mit dem Künstler stießen wir auf Parallelen unserer doch unterschiedlichen Vorstellungen. Nachdem wir ihm erläutert hatten, daß wir bei

From the very outset, our liking for the synaesthesia of the Baroque age led us to consider how artists could be involved in the creation of the new building for the Verbundnetz Gas AG. We were not thinking simply in terms of the obligatory concept of setting aside a fixed sum of money for "art in the building". We don't want a relief on the wall or a small piece of sculpture in front of the door. Instead of the usual procedure of juxtaposing various objects, we seek a complex integration of one element in another – a fusion of art and building to form a new whole. In order to find a number of artists who would participate in a limited competition, we approached the Düsseldorf art consultant Helge Achenbach. The following artists finally took part in the competition: Dieter Jung and Stephan Jung from Berlin, Joseph Kossuth from New York, Jana Milev from Berlin, Ulf Puder from Leipzig, George Sexton from Washington, D.C., and James Turrell from Flagstaff, Arizona.

In the end, James Turrell was selected. He is known for his years of work in the exploration of space and light, transparency and translucency – as demon-

1. WORK IS ON CONFERENCE CENTER LIGHTING ONLY.

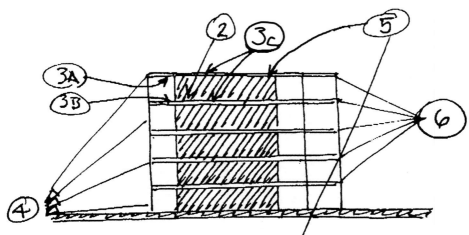

2. WORK LIGHT IN HALL AROUND CORE
3. WORK LIGHT AT OUTSIDE WALL & CEINIING JUNCTURE Ⓐ AT OUTSIDE ② WALL & FLOOR JUNCTURE Ⓑ AND WITHIN GLASS HALL WALL Ⓒ

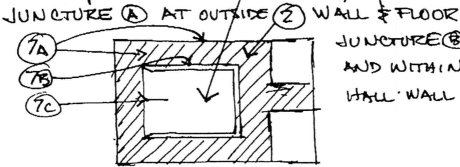

4. WORK LIGHT ON OUTSIDE GLASS IN RELATION TO INSIDE HALL LIGHT.
5. WORK LIGHT INSIDE CONFERENCE ROOM IN RELATION TO HALL LIGHT. AND IN RELATION TO OUTSIDE GLASS LIGHTING
6. WORK LIGHT ON EDGE OF STACKED FLOORS.
7. CHOOSE GLASS PATTERNING

In Modellversuchen bei der Firma Selux Berlin wurden die Leuchten entwickelt.

The light fittings were developed on the basis of tests carried out on models at the Selux company, Berlin.

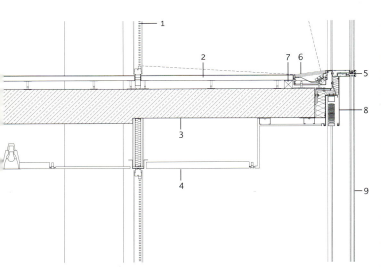

Vertikal- und Horizontalschnitt Konferenzturmfassade

1 Fassade Konferenzräume
2 Doppelboden
3 Stahlbetonflachdecke
4 Abgehängte Metallpaneeldecke, perforiert
5 Fassaden Querriegel, schallentkoppelt
6 Konferenzturmbeleuchtung Verbundsicherheitsglas rutschfest bedruckt, dreilagig Gehäusekasten Aluminiumprofil Leuchtmittel 3 Neonröhren
7 Neontrafo
8 Jalousettenkasten
9 Wärmeschutzverglasung

Vertical and horizontal sections through conference tower façade

1 façade to conference rooms
2 double-floor construction
3 reinforced concrete floor slab
4 perforated metal suspended soffit panel
5 façade rail with acoustic separation
6 conference tower lighting: three-layer laminated safety glass, non-slip printed; aluminium section housing; three neon tubes
7 neon transformer
8 blind box
9 low-E glazing

unseren Gebäuden die Erscheinung des Stofflichen auflösen möchten und mit der Architektur nach dem Immateriellen suchen, erklärte Turrell zu unserem Verblüffen, er versuche umgekehrt seit Jahren, Licht materiell erscheinen zu lassen.

Wir schlugen Turrell eine Installation für den Turm an der Nordostecke des Gebäudes vor. Dieser Bauteil dient Sitzungen, Tagungen, jeder Art von Konferenz. Mit drei Fassaden von je 14 Metern Breite und 22 Metern Höhe tritt die kubische, transparente Architektur aus dem langen Büroflügel hervor. Jede ihrer drei Seiten besteht aus einer Pfosten-Riegel-Konstruktion sowie einer inneren und einer äußeren, beide Male fast durch und durch gläsernen Wand. Dazwischen liegen auf allen sechs Geschossen Korridore. Perforierte Jalousien schirmen die Räume in der Mitte nach außen ab.

An der äußeren Seite aller Flure wurden Leuchten in die Geschoßdecken integriert. Die Installation von Turrell eignet sich die Möglichkeiten des Gebäudeleitsystems nicht funktional, sondern ästhetisch an. Digital programmiert, kann jede Neonröhre ihre Lichtfarbe verändern. Weich fließt der Ton, im Glissando von Rot über Blau nach Grün oder von Rosa über Orange nach Türkis. Er steigt auf die Unterseite der Geschoßdecken und die Lamellen der Jalousien, von wo das Licht nach draußen strömt und den Turm bei Anbruch des Abends in ein mal eher warmes, mal eher kühles, immer aber schwereloses Gebäude verwandelt.

strated in his "projection pieces" or his "skyspaces". At our very first meeting with this artist, we identified certain parallels between our concepts, despite the differences that existed. After we had explained to Turrell that we wished to dissolve the material substance of our buildings and seek an immaterial quality in the architecture, he remarked, much to our surprise, that for years he had been trying to achieve the opposite of this, namely to give light a material quality.

We suggested to Turrell that he should create an installation for the tower at the north-east corner of the building. This part of the complex is used for all kinds of meetings, discussions and conferences. With its three façades each 14 metres wide and 22 metres high, this cubic, transparent architectural element projects beyond the long eastern office tract. The three faces of the tower are in a post-and-rail construction, with an inner and an outer skin that are both almost fully glazed. Between these two layers on every floor are enclosed corridors. Perforated blinds screen the internal spaces in the tower from the outside.

On the outer edges of the corridors, light fittings were installed in the underside of the floors. Turrell's installation avails itself of the building's control and instrumentation system not in a functional manner, but aesthetically. The neon tubes are digitally programmed, so that the colour of the lighting can be individually changed. Soft tonal modulations can be achieved in glissandi that range from red, via blue to green; or from pink via orange to turquoise. The underside of the floor slabs and the louvres of the blinds are bathed in coloured light, which, flowing outwards at dusk, transforms the tower at times into a warm and at other times into a cool, but always weightless, structure.

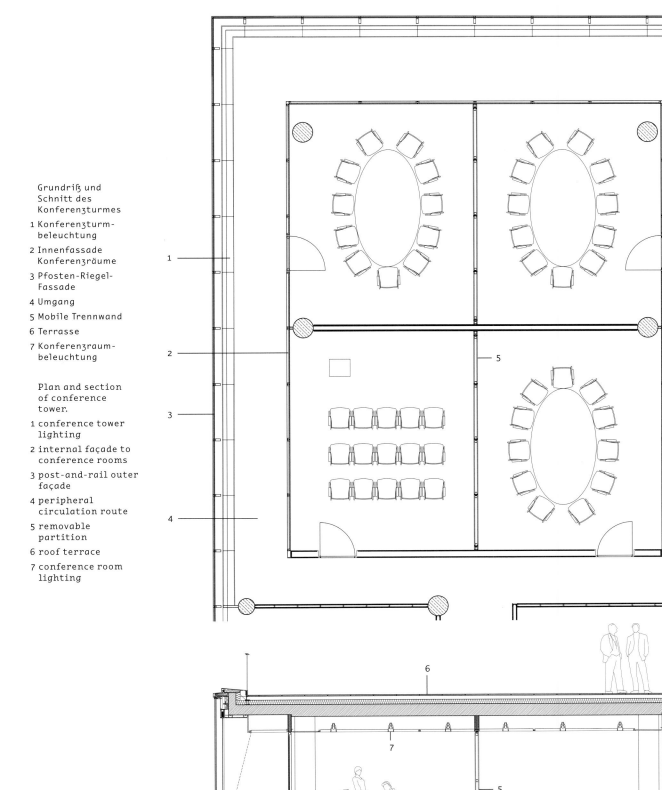

Grundriß und Schnitt des Konferenzturmes

1 Konferenzturm-beleuchtung
2 Innenfassade Konferenzräume
3 Pfosten-Riegel-Fassade
4 Umgang
5 Mobile Trennwand
6 Terrasse
7 Konferenzraum-beleuchtung

Plan and section of conference tower.

1 conference tower lighting
2 internal façade to conference rooms
3 post-and-rail outer façade
4 peripheral circulation route
5 removable partition
6 roof terrace
7 conference room lighting

Facts and figures

Daten und Fakten

Auf die Ausschreibung machten neun Unternehmen ein Angebot. Von den dabei eingegangenen 263 Änderungsvorschlägen wurden neun in das Bestellwerk aufgenommen. Nach halbjährigen Verhandlungen erhielt die Firma Dyckerhoff & Widmann, Essen und Leipzig, den Auftrag. Am 15. September 1994 begann die Arbeit auf dem Grundstück. Der Aushub des Bodens war im Januar 1995 fertig. Die 1,4 Meter dicke Stahlbetonbodenplatte wurde zwischen Februar und März 1995 gegossen. Zwischen September 1995 und März 1996 wurden 10 900 Quadratmeter gläserner Fassaden montiert. Am 3. November 1995 wurde Richtfest gefeiert. Über 1 000 Menschen aus beinahe allen Ländern Europas waren auf der Leipziger Baustelle tätig. Am 14. März 1997 zog die Verbundnetz Gas AG in ihre neue Hauptverwaltung ein.

Nine contractors submitted tenders for the construction of the works. Of the 263 proposed variations, only nine were adopted and implemented as part of the specified work. After roughly six months of negotiations, Dyckerhoff & Widmann in Essen and Leipzig were awarded the contract. On 15 September, 1994, work commenced on site. The excavation was completed in January 1995, and the 1.4-metre-thick reinforced concrete foundation slab was executed in February and March 1995. Between September 1995 and March 1996, 10,900 square metres of glazed façades were assembled. The topping-out ceremony was held on 3 November 1995. More than 1,000 people from almost all the nations of Europe were employed on the Leipzig site. On 14 March, 1997, the Verbundnetz Gas AG moved into its new headquarters.

Beteiligte Participants

Vordach am westlichen Haupteingang.

Canopy in front of main entrance in western face.

Project
Objekt: Hauptverwaltung der Verbundnetz Gas AG, Leipzig
Client
Bauherr: Immobilienfonds Bürohaus Leipzig Nordost GbR, Troisdorf
Developer
Vertreten durch: Josef Esch Fonds Projekt GmbH, Troisdorf
General assignee
Generalübernehmer: Gebrüder Esch Wohnbaugesellschaft mbH, Troisdorf
Tenant
Nutzer: Verbundnetz Gas AG, Leipzig
Architects and overall planners
Architekten und Generalplaner: Becker Gewers Kühn & Kühn Architekten, Berlin
Project team
Team: Eike Becker (verantwortlich, overall responsiblity), Georg Gewers, Oliver Kühn, Swantje Kühn, Thomas Herr (Projektleitung, project architect), Barbara Faigle, Jörn Focken, Hubert Haas, Anne Hengst, Robert Hoh, Johann Kögel, Josef Konrad, Taizo Mazuno, Oliver Mehl, Tilman Richter-von Senfft, Bettina Rosenbach, Matthias Rudolph, Susanne Schneider, Martin Wirth
Project manager
Projektsteuerer: Prof. Weiss & Partner, Oberursel
Main contractor
Generalunternehmer: Dyckerhoff & Widmann, Essen und Leipzig
Site management
Bauleitung: Sieme & Geffe Bauplanung, Berlin
Structural engineers
Tragwerkplanung: Arup GmbH, Berlin
Façades
Fassaden: Jasp Steinmetz GmbH, Nidda
Canopy
Vordach: Sobek Ingenieure GmbH, Stuttgart
Constructional physics
Bauphysik: Axel C. Rahn, Berlin
Mechanical services
Gebäudetechnik: J. Roger Preston & Partners, Maidenhead, und Klimasystemtechnik (RP+K Sozietät), Berlin
Electrical planning
Elektroplanung: Siemens AG, Berlin
Lighting planning
Lichtplanung: George Sexton Associates, Washington D.C.
Security technology
Sicherheitstechnik: Bull Ingenieurplan, Waldbronn
Fire protection
Brandschutz: Hosser, Hass & Partner, Berlin
Computer centre
Rechenzentrum: RZ Plan GmbH, München
External works
Außenanlagen: Wehberg Eppinger Schmidtke, Hamburg
Art
Kunst: James Turrell, Flagstaff/Arizona, und Achenbach Art Consulting GmbH, Düsseldorf

BGKK Biografien
BGKK biographies

Eike Becker
1962 geboren in Osterholz-Scharmbeck, Niedersachsen
1983–1990 Architekturstudium in Aachen und Stuttgart
1989–1990 DAAD Stipendium Ecole d'Architecture Belleville, Paris
1990 Diplom TU Stuttgart
1990–1991 Norman Foster Associates, London
1991 Richard Rogers Partnership, London
1997 Gründung der Gesellschaft für zeitgenössische Kunst, Berlin
    Teilnahme an der documenta X, Kassel
1998 Teilnahme an der berlin biennale für zeitgenössische Kunst
1999 Vorstand der Kunst-Werke, Berlin
Born in 1962 in Osterholz-Scharmbeck, Lower Saxony
1983–90 Studied architecture in Aachen and Stuttgart
1989–90 DAAD scholarship to Ecole d'Architecture Belleville, Paris
1990 Diploma at University of Technology, Stuttgart
1990–91 Norman Foster Associates, London
1991 Richard Rogers Partnership, London
1997 Founding of Gesellschaft für zeitgenössische Kunst, Berlin
    Participation at documenta X, Kassel
1998 Participation at berlin biennale for contemporary art
1999 Board of Kunst-Werke, Berlin

Georg Gewers
1962 geboren in Bevergern, Westfalen
1978–1982 Bildhauerausbildung bei Bernd Gewers
1983–1990 Architekturstudium in Aachen und Stuttgart
1987–1989 Büroerfahrung in Stuttgart und Osnabrück
1989–1990 DAAD Stipendium Ecole d'Architecture Belleville, Paris
1990 Diplom TU Stuttgart
1990–1991 Norman Foster Associates, London
Born in 1962 in Bevergern, Westphalia
1978–82 Trained as sculptor with Bernd Gewers
1983–90 Studied architecture in Aachen and Stuttgart
1987–89 Worked in offices in Stuttgart and Osnabrück
1989–90 DAAD scholarship to Ecole d'Architecture Belleville, Paris
1990 Diploma at University of Technology, Stuttgart
1990–91 Norman Foster Associates, London

Oliver Kühn
1962 geboren in Regensburg
1983–1988 Architekturstudium in München
1988 Diplom TU München
1989 Büroerfahrung in München
1989–1991 Richard Rogers Partnership, London
1991 Consultant Richard Rogers Partnership, Berlin
1998–1999 Managementstudium, St. Gallen, Schweiz
Born in 1962 in Regensburg
1983–88 Studied architecture in Munich
1988 Diploma at University of Technology, Munich
1989 Office experience in Munich
1989–91 Richard Rogers Partnership, London
1991 Consultant Richard Rogers Partnership, Berlin
1998–1999 Studied business administration, St. Gallen, Switzerland

Swantje Kühn
1964 geboren in München
1983 Bachelor of Arts, Wesleyan University, Illinois, USA
1983–1989 Architekturstudium in München
1986 Projekte für die Gesellschaft für Technische Zusammenarbeit in Malawi, Afrika
1989 Diplom TU München
1989–1991 Richard Rogers Partnership, London
1998 Anwendungsspezialist Bauinformatik, Bauakademie Berlin
Born in 1964 in Munich
1983 Bachelor of Arts, Wesleyan University, Illinois, USA
1983–89 Studied architecture in Munich
1986 Projects for the GtZ in Malawi, Africa
1989 Diploma at University of Technology, Munich
1989–91 Richard Rogers Partnership, London
1998 Construction computer applications specialist, Bauakademie Berlin

Bis April 1994 hatten wir unser Büro an der Schnittstelle von West und Ost, im ehemaligen Grandhotel Esplanade an der Bellevuestraße. Ein Aussichtsturm aus Mauerzeiten, ein Souvenirladen, das Weinhaus Huth, der leere Potsdamer und Leipziger Platz, der Tiergarten, die Staatsbibliothek und das Brandenburger Tor bildeten unsere Nachbarschaft. Besprechungen mit Bauherren führten wir im »Kaisersaal« durch, den Sony später als Ganzes verschob.

Up to April 1994, our office was located at the interface between West and East, in the former Grand Hotel Esplanade in Bellevuestrasse, Berlin. An observation tower from the time of the Berlin Wall, a souvenir shop, the Huth wine tavern, the empty space of Potsdamer Platz and Leipziger Platz, the Tiergarten, the State Library and the Brandenburg Gate were all in the immediate neighbourhood. Our discussions with clients took place in the "Kaisersaal", a structure that was later moved by Sony en bloc to a different position.

Ausstellungen
Exhibitions
1995
→ Galerie Aedes East, Berlin
1996
→ Galerie am Weißenhof, Stuttgart

Auszeichnungen
Prizes and awards
1997
→ Bauherrenpreis Modernisierung für die Sophie-Gips-Höfe Sammlung Hoffmann, Berlin
1998
→ Deubau Preis für die Hauptverwaltung der Verbundnetz Gas AG, Leipzig
→ Anerkennung Balthasar-Neumann-Preis für die Hauptverwaltung der Verbundnetz Gas AG, Leipzig
→ Anerkennung Gestaltungspreis der Wüstenrot Stiftung für die Sophie-Gips-Höfe Sammlung Hoffmann, Berlin

Wettbewerbe ab 1996
Competitions since 1996
1996
→ Eingeladener Realisierungswettbewerb Vista-Business-Center Berlin-Adlershof, Zweiter Preis
1997
→ Eingeladenes Gutachterverfahren Neues Stadtteilzentrum Regensburg-Burgweinting, Erster Preis
→ Eingeladenes Gutachterverfahren Altmarkt Dresden, Zweiter Preis
1998
→ Eingeladener Realisierungswettbewerb Fabbrica Arte Contemporanea Turin, Zweiter Preis
→ Eingeladener Realisierungswettbewerb Hauptverwaltung der Television Arte Straßburg, Zweiter Preis
→ Eingeladener Realisierungswettbewerb Rhodarium im Bürgerpark Bremen, Zweiter Preis
1999
→ Eingeladener Realisierungswettbewerb Hauptverwaltung der Lufthansa AG, Frankfurt am Main, Vierter Preis

Bauten bis 2000
Buildings up to 2000
1993
→ Um- und Neubau Rethmann Data-Recycling-Anlage, Werneuchen
1994
→ Neubau Raiffeisenbank, Zossen
1996
→ Neubau Wohnpark Friedrichsthal, Schwerin
1997
→ Um- und Neubau Sophie-Gips-Höfe Sammlung Hoffmann, Berlin
→ Neubau Hauptverwaltung der Verbundnetz Gas AG, Leipzig
1998
→ Neubau Wohnhäuser Rummelsburger Bucht, Berlin
1999/2000
→ Neubau MTU Motoren- und Turbinen-Union Kunden- und Schulungszentrum, Ludwigsfelde
→ Umbau Empfangshalle Hauptbahnhof, Frankfurt/Oder
→ Umbau Empfangshalle Ostbahnhof, Berlin
→ Neubau Verbändehaus Friedrichstadt, Berlin
→ Um- und Neubau Brauerei-Schultheiß-Areal zum Wohn- und Kulturpark, Berlin

Projekte ab 1999
Projekts since 1999
→ Umbau Alter Speicher Stralau, Berlin
→ Umbau Wohnhochhaus Märkische Allee, Berlin
→ Umbau Wohnhochhaus Helene-Weigel-Platz, Berlin
→ Neubau Wohnhaus Auguststraße, Berlin
→ Neubau Hotelhochhaus Messedamm, Berlin
→ Neubau Büro- und Geschäftshaus Friedrichcarré, Berlin
→ Neubau Pavillon der Bertelsmann AG Expo 2000, Hannover mit Triad Architekten, Berlin
→ Neubau Stadthalle Oelde, Oelde
→ Neubau Pavillons Landesgartenschau Nordrhein-Westfalen 2001, Oelde

Bibliographie
Bibliography

Aedes East (Hrsg.)
Mix_t, Becker Gewers Kühn & Kühn Architekten, Katalog der Ausstellung in der Galerie Aedes East Berlin, Berlin 1995

Crossing, Gespräch mit Eike Becker und Georg Gewers
in: Deutsche Bauzeitung 11/1995

Becker Gewers Kühn & Kühn Architekten BDA, Projekte und Bauten 1992–1995, Wiesbaden 1996

Christian Brensing
Berlin Young Architects Today II,
in: Architectural Design 9/10/1996

Helga Hoffmann
Die sanfte Tour, Hauptverwaltung der Verbundnetz Gas AG, Ein Gespräch mit Eike Becker
in: Intelligente Architektur 5/1996

Joachim Goetz
Architektur soll unterhalten wie ein guter Film, Becker Gewers Kühn & Kühn in der Architekturgalerie am Stuttgarter Weißenhof
in: Stuttgarter Zeitung 8.6.1996

Wolfgang Bachmann
Verwaltung der Verbundnetz Gas AG in Leipzig
in: Baumeister 5/1997

Die Zukunft ist digital, Elf Fragen an Eike Becker
in: Baumeister 5/1997

Eike Becker
Hauptverwaltung der Verbundnetz Gas AG in Leipzig
in: Glas, Architektur und Technik 3/1997

Dietmar Danner
Symbiose
in: Intelligente Architektur 8/1997

Anna Klingmann
Differenzierte Transparenz
in: Deutsche Bauzeitung 11/1997

Eike Becker
Hauptverwaltung der Verbundnetz Gas AG
in: Peter Neitzke u.a. (Hrsg.), Centrum, Jahrbuch Architektur und Stadt 1997/1998, Braunschweig und Wiesbaden 1997

Carl Steckeweh und Reinhart Wustlich (Hrsg.)
Im Grundsatz: Modern, Deubau Junior Award 1998, Architekturpreis für junge Architektinnen und Architekten, Darmstadt 1998

Claus Käpplinger
High-Tech mit Eleganz
in: Foyer 3/1998

Anerkennung Bürogebäude Hauptverwaltung der Verbundnetz Gas AG Leipzig
in: Deutsche Bauzeitung, Balthasar-Neumann-Preis 1998, Sonderheft 1998

Ingeborg Flagge
Hauptverwaltung der Verbundnetz Gas AG
in: Engelbert Lütke-Daldrup (Hrsg.), Leipzig Bauten 1989-1999, Basel u.a.O. 1999

Dank
Acknowledgements

Unser Dank gilt folgenden Personen:
We should like to express our thanks to the following persons:

Eckhard Becker
Johannes Determann
Stefan Doman
Wolfgang F. Eschment
Werner Fischer
Jörn Focken
Horst Friedemann
Udo Gerbracht
Thomas Glatter
David Glover
Dr.-Ing. Werner Hauenherm
Dietmar Hebenstreit
Thomas Herr
Dr.-Ing. Klaus-Ewald Holst
Dr.-Ing. Axel Jahn
Werner Keutmann
Friedrich Kühn
Ian Mulquiny
Dr. Karl-Heinz Schubert
George Sexton
Horst Steinmetz
Derek Tuddenham
James Turrell
Prof. Walter Weiss
Martin Wirth
Egbert Wodrich
Dr. Johannes Wolf
Prof. Dr. Gerhardt Wolff